RUNNING FOR MY LIFE

RUNNING
FOR MY
LIFE

JORDAN WYLIE

Biteback Publishing

First published in Great Britain in 2019 by
Biteback Publishing Ltd
Westminster Tower
3 Albert Embankment
London SE1 7SP
Copyright © Jordan Wylie 2019

ISBN 978-1-78590-526-1

10 9 8 7 6 5 4 3 2 1

A CIP catalogue record for this book is available from the British Library.

Set in Minion Pro

Printed and bound in Great Britain by
CPI Group (UK) Ltd, Croydon CR0 4YY

This book is dedicated to all the innocent children worldwide who have suffered injury, death or trauma as a result of war and conflict.

CONTENTS

Acknowledgements ix

Maps xi

Foreword xv

Chapter One: Up on the Roof 1

Chapter Two: The Injured Soldier 5

Chapter Three: A Broken Man 25

Chapter Four: The Black Dog 43

Chapter Five: Quarantined 59

Chapter Six: A Growth Mindset 67

Chapter Seven: The Shock of Seizure 81

Chapter Eight: Keep Moving Forwards 89

Chapter Nine: Exercise is the Best Medicine 99

Chapter Ten: The World's Most Dangerous Place 113

Chapter Eleven: An Undiscovered Beauty 137

Chapter Twelve: Irony   147
Chapter Thirteen: The Ultimate Victims of War   157
Chapter Fourteen: Back to Iraq   165
Chapter Fifteen: The Land of the Taliban   189
Chapter Sixteen: Beautiful Bamiyan   219
Chapter Seventeen: Be the Difference that   233
                      Makes a Difference

About the Author   253

ACKNOWLEDGEMENTS

My grateful thanks are due to the following people:

To all the people of Somalia, Somaliland, Iraq and Afghanistan. I will never forget the kind, genuine and warm hospitality you showed me while I passed through your homelands. It was a privilege and an honour to meet you all and I hope that one day you all find the peace and happiness you very much deserve from this world.

To legendary athlete Dai Greene, for writing the foreword for this book and for providing inspiration through his performance and actions on and off the track. And for showing me that as long as you believe it and are prepared to make the sacrifices, you can achieve anything you wish in life.

To Sandra Cain, who has worked side by side with me and helped greatly over the last twelve months by skilfully extracting all my memories to bring this journey together: the good, the bad and the extremely ugly in some cases. You have taken me back to places I didn't think I would ever revisit and have helped me – more than you will ever know – to deal with issues deep within me. Thank you so much from the bottom of my heart. I am very proud to call you my friend.

To everyone at Biteback Publishing who believed in me right from our initial interactions. There was something quite magical and serendipitous about how our paths crossed and it was clearly meant to be. I am especially grateful to James Stephens, Olivia Beattie and Namkwan Cho for their close cooperation and unwavering support, which has allowed me to share my latest adventure with the world.

To all the incredible children of the world living in conflict and war zones, I sincerely hope that peace, security, education and healthcare will one day be part of your normality. I will continue to pray for this daily...

I would like to express my gratitude to Stephen McGrath for the excellent cover photo and also to cartographer Alice Gadney, from Silver7 Mapping, for the admirable work she has kindly created at the front of this book which brings my story to life.

Finally, I would like to give a huge shout-out to all my magnificent sponsors and supporters. Your faith in me and in my personal adventures to help others has been astonishing to date and I thank you all.

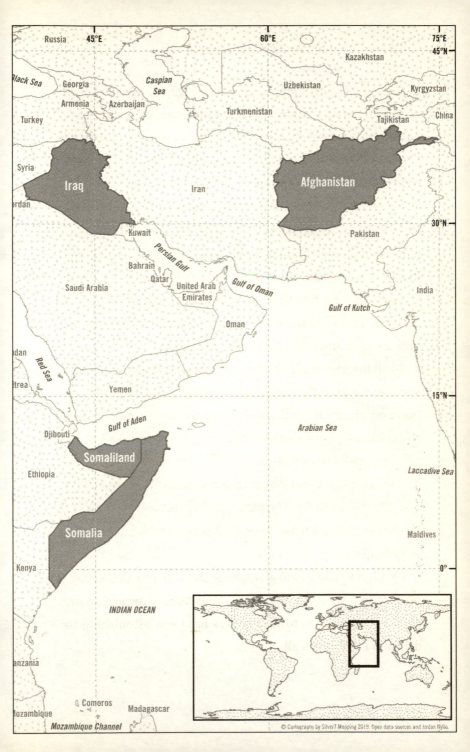

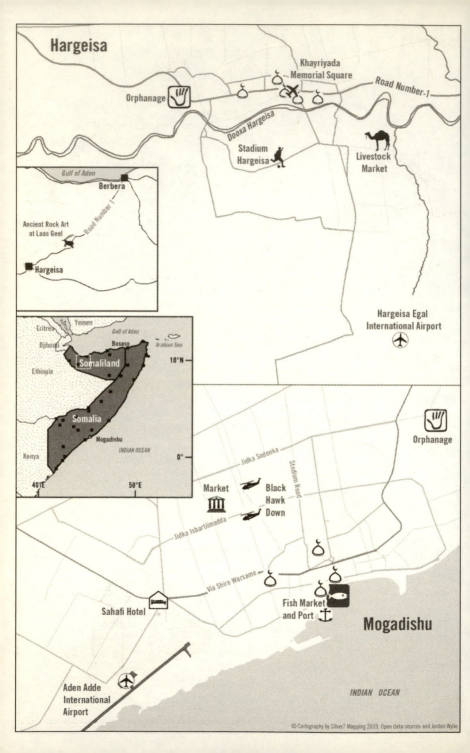

Hargeisa

Khayriyada
Memorial Square

Road Number-1

Orphanage

Dooxa Hargeisa

Stadium
Hargeisa

Livestock
Market

Gulf of Aden

Berbera

Road Number 1

Ancient Rock Art
at Laas Geel

Hargeisa

Hargeisa Egal
International Airport

Yemen

Eritrea

Djibouti

Gulf of Aden

Bosaso

Arabian Sea

Somaliland

10°N

Ethiopia

Somalia

Mogadishu

Kenya

INDIAN OCEAN

0°

40°E

50°E

Orphanage

Jidka Sodonka

Stadium Road

Market

Black
Hawk
Down

Jidka Isbartiimadda

Via Shire Warsame

Sahafi Hotel

Fish Market
and Port

Mogadishu

Aden Adde
International
Airport

INDIAN OCEAN

© Cartography by Silver7 Mapping 2019. Open data sources and Jordan Wylie

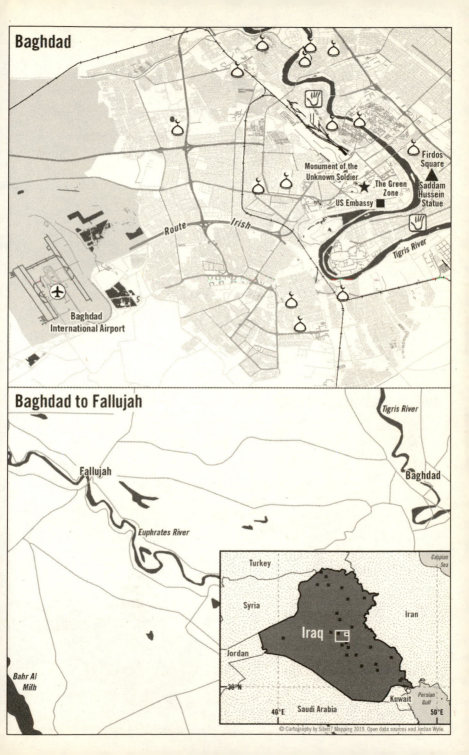

Baghdad

Monument of the
Unknown Soldier

The Green
Zone

US Embassy

Firdos
Square

Saddam
Hussein
Statue

Route Irish

Tigris River

Baghdad
International Airport

Baghdad to Fallujah

Tigris River

Fallujah

Baghdad

Euphrates River

Bahr Al
Milh

Turkey

Caspian
Sea

Syria

Iran

Iraq

Jordan

30°N

40°E

Saudi Arabia

Kuwait

Persian
Gulf

50°E

© Cartography by Silver7 Mapping 2019. Open data sources and Jordan Wylie.

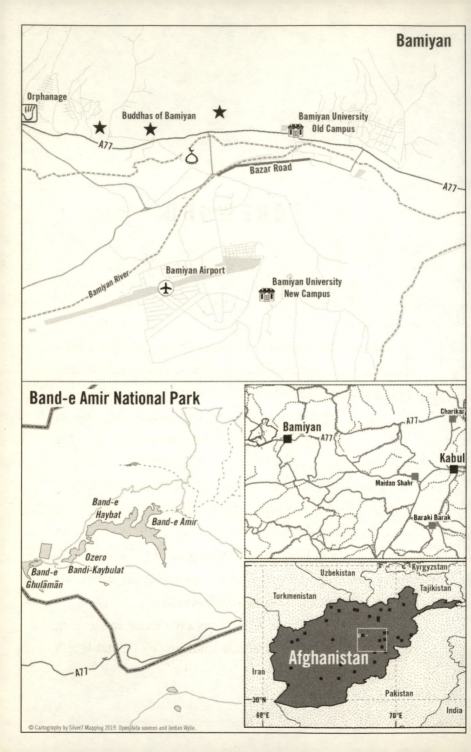

Bamiyan

Orphanage

A77

Buddhas of Bamiyan

★

★

★

Bazar Road

Bamiyan University
Old Campus

A77

Bamiyan River

Bamiyan Airport

Bamiyan University
New Campus

Band-e Amir National Park

Band-e
Haybat

Band-e Amir

Ozero
Bandi-Kaybulat

Band-e
Ghulāmān

A77

Charikar

Bamiyan

A77

Kabul

Maidan Shahr

Baraki Barak

Kyrgyzstan

Uzbekistan

Tajikistan

Turkmenistan

Afghanistan

Iran

30°N

60°E

Pakistan

70°E

India

© Cartography by Silver7 Mapping 2019. Open data sources and Jordan Wylie.

FOREWORD

It takes a vast amount of determination and grit to face what look like insurmountable obstacles when you are challenged by both mental and physical issues. *Running for My Life* is a true story of endurance and tenacity against the odds. It is the story of one man's mission to bring awareness of the plight of children suffering in war and conflict zones and to raise much-needed funds to inspire hope for their futures through education and opportunity. To do this, Jordan Wylie, a former British soldier turned extreme adventurer, chose to train and run in what the UK Foreign and Commonwealth Office determine are three of the world's most dangerous countries – Somalia, Iraq and Afghanistan.

But what made these three runs even more challenging is the fact that Jordan is affected not just by mental health issues from his experiences, but also with epilepsy. Having epilepsy myself, I understand and have first-hand knowledge of how debilitating this condition can be. Like me, Jordan had to overcome self-doubt and the doubt of others before transforming his life and pushing on forward to make his mark on the world. Jordan's story busts many of the myths in society today and shows what can be achieved with self-belief, risk management and fortitude. Braving the ever present threat of logistical crises, Taliban insurgents, stultifying heat, fierce terrain and nose-bleed-inducing altitude, the injured British Army veteran pushed on.

Running for My Life highlights the willpower necessary to endure well beyond the perceived limitations of psychological and physical human endurance. But it's not just a story of determination and grit – it's more than that – it's a story of the grace and simplicity that can be found in communities whose own hardships far outweigh our own. It's a story of the strength and kindness that is found in people whose lives are torn apart by conflict and war, it's a story of personal pride in one's own country and commitment to making a better world. Jordan's personal journey introduces us to the lives of children who are confronted by the lack of things we take for granted: education, safety, security and peace. Ultimately, it's a story of determination, gratitude, the kindness of strangers and the willingness of people to help others along the way.

As well as a thought-provoking read, *Running for My Life* is a lesson for all about how to meet challenges head-on from a man whose passion for adventure and helping others knows no boundaries.

Dai Greene, World, European and Commonwealth Champion

CHAPTER ONE

UP ON THE ROOF

I was pacing the roof of a ninety-storey skyscraper, gulping air like a fish out of water. My feet had taken on a perverse life of their own. My eyes fixed on the spread of glittering buildings below and the starkness of the sand dunes beyond. I was just about holding it together, desperately searching for some peace and quiet far away from the crushing claustrophobia of Dubai. I badly needed relief from the screaming pain in my own head, the endless honking of cars and the chronic madness of the city below. I was at the lowest point in my life.

I stared helplessly at my phone. Several disenchanted texts and emails glared angrily back. A heavy feeling of dread whirled round in the spin cycle of my brain. I'd been up on that roof for the whole day and a full night thinking, 'How can I solve this, how can I fix this?' I'd let everyone down, my ex-fiancée Laura, my daughter Evie, my parents and my personal code of honour. I'd used up all of my lifelines with my ex. Now, I just wanted to puke my guts up because I'd hurt everyone and everything I loved and cared for. I'd never felt so much pain in my life. My head was clamped in a vice and about to burst open and splatter gore all over the deck.

My mobile rang. I looked at it lying like a malignant slab of terror in the palm of my hand and saw the familiar name light up, alerting me to the caller. I clamped the phone tightly to my ear as my stomach fell away to my feet. 'You bastard, you absolute fucking useless bastard!' I winced as Laura yelled down the phone at me, calling me every rotten name under the sun. 'I'm sick to death of you, Jordan. You let me down again and again, it's relentless and I've had enough. I can't take it. I just don't know how to cope with you any more.' I listened wordlessly and then cancelled the call.

I deserved it all… every insult and every hateful retort. I loathed myself; I'd let down the very people I cared about, those I respected and loved more than anything. But most of all, I'd let myself down and gone against all the values I measured my life against. I'd renounced the integrity, the loyalty, the respect for others, the courage, the selfless commitment and the discipline I'd learned and taken to heart in the military. I'd gone against everything I believed I stood for and got myself caught up in an endless circle of damaging emotion.

The army had instilled the importance of personal values in me – the specific beliefs that people have about what's important and unimportant in life and the way one should conduct oneself. My values underpinned the basis of trust that people had in me and I in them. Now, I'd gone and broken that trust. I no longer deserved to be seen by others as a good man. What good man would behave the way I had? I was never a cheat or a liar, but my priorities in life were all wrong. I wasn't leading by example, I wasn't applying discipline, I wasn't encouraging confidence, I wasn't striving for team goals. I'd allowed myself to become weak and diminished. As I looked towards the horizon, I felt how easy it would be to just launch myself over the rooftop towards oblivion.

'Get a grip, man, get a fucking grip, will you?' I whispered to myself, alternatively trying to sort the other side of the argument. I'd always been a lover of life and a celebrant of the pure joy of being alive. This shit I was going through right now was a total pisser to say the least. A few floors below me, sitting in relative comfort and ignorance of my plight were several of my colleagues who were working with me in the maritime security industry. We all shared an apartment. None of them knew I was up here and no doubt none of them missed me; they were too busy watching the sports channels or scrolling through Twitter or Facebook. I was alone – just me and my crazy mind.

I'd used the wide emergency exit and maintenance back stairs to climb to the roof, a dank, dark and lonely stairwell completely out of keeping with the glitz of Dubai. Now, high up on the rooftop, I was left looking at the glamour below, the super-modern architecture, the chrome pillars and the blue strobe lighting, the luxurious hotels, the big, flash, shiny cars… and the hidden, silent deprivation beyond.

The untold stories of Filipino and Bangladeshi taxi drivers who have their passports confiscated on arrival, the tales of Indian nationals sleeping ten to a room behind a flimsy curtain, the sex slaves brought in from Eastern Europe, they all spoke to me. I felt complete empathy with their compromised humanity. I couldn't relate to the luxury of Dubai. The more I thought about my life, my own hopes and dreams and the hopes and dreams of those I loved, the worse I felt. The reality was my partner was going her own way and taking my daughter with her and I was going to be left stewing in my own shit. I'd been up on that roof for a whole day and a night, arguing with myself about whether to end my pain quickly. It was just a step away…

CHAPTER TWO

THE INJURED SOLDIER

I never achieved much at school, although I was great at sports, even if I do say so myself. Football was my game, but then so were basketball, cricket and athletics. I loved anything to do with a ball. Being the captain of the team, I thought I was pretty cool because to me, sport was everything, and I took every opportunity to get involved. I wasn't a total academic loser, but I was a bit of a Jack the Lad in the classroom. On reflection, I realise I was probably a juvenile idiot and my behaviour was undoubtedly irritating and disruptive. I probably got on a lot of people's nerves. I was always the one up for a laugh, the one charming the ladies, the one who never thought very far into the future. Instant gratification was my number one rule; I hated having to wait for anything. I spent a lot of time staring out the window daydreaming or missing school altogether, hanging around the back of the old bike sheds with other guys intent on bunking off. I seemed to get away with a lot just because I was a half-decent football player who knew how to find the back of the net each week, which made me popular with the other kids. I was a bit of a teacher's pet because I had a way with words and a quick smile for anyone in authority. But I was also quite naïve, a tad arrogant and convinced a glittering future lay ahead for me as a professional footballer. A bit of a tosser when you come to think of it.

The day we went into school to get our GCSE results all the students were ripping open their personalised envelopes, eager to get their grades. I hung back, embarrassed, and not looking forward to reading my results. Everyone was like, 'Hey, look how well I've done, look where I'm going next.' They were excited about this sixth-form college here or that new academy in Blackpool. I peeked in my envelope… 'Well, I ain't going nowhere!' I'd taken eleven GCSEs and managed to pass two of them with C grades, one of which was construction, and for which my dad did most of the project work. He'd helped me build one of those football tables you see in a pub or bar. I was dead proud of it. The other GCSE was for physical education, which I passed basically because I could just kick, throw and bowl a ball on a pitch or court.

I was just a lad from a council estate in Lancashire who had no fucking idea what he was going to do. I wasn't going to uni, that was a definite. I was pretty good at chatting up the ladies, getting into the odd scrap and a good laugh in the classroom, but that was hardly anything to crow about. I was stumped. Apart from footie, what else was I any good at? Had I known what the future held in store for me, I would have laughed my head off.

Sadly, reality soon came knocking and I realised I was never going to be a pro footballer. It was all wishful thinking, a gold-plated fantasy. I was sixteen years old and I had no plans for the rest of my life – or even the near future. Going into the military was a simple process of elimination. With zero decent qualifications, I wasn't really up to anything else. I probably couldn't even have got a job stacking shelves in the local supermarket and I didn't yet have a driving licence, so couldn't even cut it as a delivery driver. The more I thought about it, the more I realised what a great idea the military would be – plenty of time for sports, plus I would get to see the world, have adventures and meet new people. What wasn't to like? At least my dad would be pleased.

When the Twin Towers were attacked by the Islamist terrorist group al-Qaeda and collapsed in New York on 11 September 2001, I watched the drama unfold on the BBC. I was hanging around at a friend's house, sitting on the sofa, eating a Domino's pizza with my mouth open in disbelief and my chicken and sweetcorn slice suspended in mid-air. Me and my mate just gawped at each other, not really understanding the consequences of this atrocity, but aware it meant something very bad indeed.

Worldwide security changed dramatically as a result: airports frantically increased their screening measures and the public become hyper-vigilant. It was under these heightened security circumstances that I went off to serve in the British Army. I wasn't exactly thrilled at the thought of going to fight a war and, if I'm completely honest, at the back of my mind I never really thought I would have to. I just wanted to play football in the army and make new mates. Sitting on that plane on the way to Iraq, not long after joining up, was a massive reality check. All I could think was, 'Bloody hell, this shit is real!' Pictures on the news of guys getting blown to smithereens in the very place I was travelling to consumed me. But it was too late. I'd made my choice and here I was… a bona fide trooper in the finest cavalry regiment in history, the King's Royal Hussars – and I was still just a spotty-faced teenager with no idea about anything in life that really mattered.

The military took ten years of my life. I did two tours of Iraq, a tour of Northern Ireland and travelled the world, visiting Poland, Cyprus, Germany, Canada, the USA and the Falklands. My own father had served in the Falklands back in '82 with Her Majesty's Royal Marines, so being able to trace his footsteps meant something very special to me. I admired my dad enormously and his sense of integrity inspired me. I always wanted him to be proud of me.

I was honoured to serve with the King's Royal Hussars (KRH), a regiment with over 300 years of history which started on horseback and evolved over generations to serve in what is known today as the Challenger 2 main battle tank. There is something pretty special about charging around the battlefield in sixty-two tonnes of armour, and I never really understood why they would let a seventeen-year-old kid take responsibility for driving a multimillion-pound killing machine. I'd crashed my Vauxhall Corsa enough times in the last six months so it was a pretty big ask, expecting me to take charge of one of the British Army's most powerful bits of equipment.

Although I was trained in all the roles of full crewman on the Challenger 2, I quickly found my passion was in working with much smaller vehicles within a specialist section in my unit called Close Reconnaissance Troop. Our job was paramount to success in combat as we were responsible for preparing the way for the rest of the force. We would spend most of our time in a covert capacity out in front, carrying out many different roles, from scouting for information to engaging enemy targets. Reconnaissance, or 'recce' as we would call ourselves, was an essential element for gathering information and intelligence by stealth, both on foot and from our specialist vehicles, Scimitars. We trained in many different environments, from the baking desert and the freezing Arctic to the unforgiving jungle, and I thoroughly enjoyed my time there. I still reflect on this period as certainly one of the highlights in my military career. I was a proud recce soldier and I made some great friends who I still see today. When you work in very small teams, you build on already high levels of trust and integrity, and for optimum performance on operations you have to be able to trust every man in your troop. I don't mind saying we were pretty damn good at what we did, which is why we were selected to be the best of the best at the time in the regiment.

In my early days on duty, I was still learning but had certainly lost the arrogance and cocky know-it-all teenage attitude that arrived with me on day one of basic training. The instructors don't mess about when it comes to discipline; they teach you the hard way and you can't pull the wool over these guys' eyes. They're the best in the business and have been hand-picked for their role as recruit training staff. Most of the corporals and sergeants you meet in basic also came from tough backgrounds, so they tend to have seen it all before and don't have much sympathy for anyone's case. We were soldiers now and we were all equals. The lessons I learned in military training have served me well in life.

The army sent me to the Defence Intelligence Centre in Bedfordshire, to a place called Chicksands, where I trained for a military intelligence course, finishing as the top student in my small intake. For some reason, I found I was pretty good at it. I wasn't the best soldier in the world, or even the regiment or squadron for that matter, but I seemed to excel at this intelligence stuff. It was an eye-opener, and I felt a great sense of achievement and satisfaction. My bad attitude to school began to fade into the background. Here was something, apart from sport, I could excel at – and more importantly, something I enjoyed.

I ended up as a 'prisoner handler, tactical questioner and interrogator'. Quite a mouthful, but basically, I built profiles on key enemy commanders by extracting information from the bad guys lower down the chain that we had captured to use for counter-insurgency terrorism operations. I got to embed myself in the lives of others, working out what makes them tick and looking for any vulnerabilities we could exploit. I was only a lance corporal, which is very low down the pecking order in the chain of command, being only one up above a private or a 'trooper' as we called them in the Royal Armoured Corps. I wasn't at the strategic level as such, but because I was working in a very niche intelligence cell, I was obviously accessing a lot more information than your average soldier, so I was part of the analytical process. We would identify targets, gather information and intelligence and then present it to senior commanders who would assess the next course of action.

The intelligence cycle is one of processing information in military or law enforcement. The stages of the intelligence cycle include all the necessary requirements needed by the decision makers. We'd study and analyse the *direction* given from senior commanders and from there we would formulate plans to send out. The next phase of the cycle would be *collection*. That could be anything from researching open-source materials online, or it could be sending out a military patrol to identify a target, a position, a person or simply a building. We'd gather all sorts of data, perhaps we'd look at how busy a certain road junction is between twelve and three o'clock in the afternoon, or what a particular man is wearing, or how busy the market is on a Thursday, or what vehicles are entering a certain garage. It could be anything, a million different things really, context was everything. We would then collate all the information we had gathered. The third phase of the intelligence cycle is *processing*. Here we put all the pieces of the jigsaw together to try and analyse it and come to some conclusions where we could then make an intelligence assessment. For example, why does that particular man go into a certain house at eleven o'clock every Thursday and why does that particular driver hand over a package to a woman with a pram every morning, or why is that roundabout before the market always empty on a Sunday morning? We call this 'understanding the pattern of life' and from this we're able to see if there are any changes with important implications for safety and security. For example, if we know the market in Baghdad is busy every Thursday between 12.00 and 5.00 p.m. because they have a sale on cattle, for example, and if one day at 12.00 to 5.00 p.m. that market is completely empty, we know something's not right. There's a change in the behaviour of the pattern of life. Call it a presence of the abnormal and an absence of the normal. That might give us a potential combat indicator, meaning something bad was likely to happen. We'd disseminate our findings back to the strategic commanders. This intelligence would then be used to coordinate our patrols, our operations and hopefully, ultimately, defeat the enemy.

I learned a hell of a lot about human motivations and what drives a person to do what they do. Motivation is an internal process that makes a person move towards a goal. Motivation, like intelligence, can't be directly observed. Instead, motivation can only be inferred by noting a person's behaviour. I got to practise superior questioning skills, pull lots of psychological levers, assess and exploit weaknesses and extract important information. My colleagues and I played a lot of good cop, bad cop stuff, making emotional connections and building rapport to get what we wanted – a skill that came in handy when in later years I was asked to be one of the 'hunters' on Channel Four's BAFTA-nominated and award-winning *Hunted* and *Celebrity Hunted* TV shows.

Working in intelligence was both a highly frustrating and rewarding experience. Rightly so, there was always a human rights expert or someone from the UN standing next to me and my colleagues in the interrogation room, watching us work. But it bugged me that frequently, I would be questioning a known terrorist – who may or may not have been responsible for the deaths of several British soldiers – and an ex-military man working for the UN would interrupt to tersely inform me that I'd been interrogating for thirty minutes and it was now time to stop and offer the prisoner a drink of water. There would also be regular stops for food, which really wound me up because as far as I could see this potential terrorist was getting better treatment than the soldiers on the ground.

The military is built on an ethos of teamwork and ethics, values which have marked my life. It's so much more than 'queen and country', it's about bringing home the whole team from operations or patrol. When you're on ops, you're living cheek by jowl, totally reliant on another person for your life and vice versa. That sort of personal commitment breathes life into long-term relationships. I'm not sure civilians can ever quite comprehend the importance and power of the depth of military relationships. There's a bond – that old cliché of a 'band of brothers' – which guarantees you'll always be there for each other. If there's one take-away from my army days, it's the three maxims my old commanding officer banged into me. One: we're all one big team. Two: always think things through to the finish and don't leave a job half done. Three: do as you ought and not as you want. That last one speaks to me the most. Sometimes, you just have to do the right thing and not what you want to do.

To me, having values and standards are a core part of who I am today, what I do and why I set out to help others through my charitable endeavours. Soldiering in a war zone had made a profound impact on me in terms of appreciating how little some people have in life and how their lives are limited by fear and risk. But it was the plight of the children in these war zones that affected me the most (and even more so after becoming a father myself). After all, no child ever started a war, but it's they who suffer the most when the adults start fighting over resources, politics, religion and money. They are the ones who are the innocent and ultimate victims of war. They have no influence, no control and no recourse.

I felt sorry for the people of Iraq. I saw scenes of violence and separation that sat badly with me. The Iraqis had to live with this every single day of their lives. I was in Iraq for only six months at a time and I couldn't wait to get back and hold Mum and Dad tight. War is not glamorous, it's not exciting, it's dehumanising and desperate. I kept a calendar on a small wooden cabinet by the bed in my shared tent and ticked off each day in relief as it ended. I was literally counting the days off one by one until I could leave the country and get back home to sanity, safety and the people I loved.

Although I enjoyed my job in intelligence, I didn't so much enjoy the restrictions of living in an army camp. We were not allowed to leave, even if we wanted to – which we sure as hell didn't. It was bloody dangerous out there. Our camp was bombarded constantly with mortars and rockets almost every night for the six months I was there. I saw horrific injuries including crushed bodies, limbs blown off and, inevitably, death. The local Iraqis just wanted to live normal lives, going to work and caring for their families, despite the pandemonium and chaos surrounding them. When I saw how the children suffered, I wanted to pick them up and take them home with me. I was incredibly affected by their sweetness, their sorrow and their trust. The simplest things, such as carrying sweets and bottles of fresh water with us on patrol and handing them out to the kids, made their day.

As a soldier in any war zone, you come across local children on a daily basis. More often than not they are intrigued by who you are and what you are doing; they are often smiling or laughing and just want to innocently interact with you, the way young children often do. They reminded me of myself as a child – a bit cheeky, always up for fun and a bit of adventure. I guess they were used to seeing guns, tanks, artillery shells and the like in their streets. War was very much a normal part of an otherwise brutal life for some children.

Once, on my second tour of Iraq, we were heading out to a meeting with some tribal leaders on the Iran/Iraq border and while we were in the meeting with the village elders, several children were outside on the side of the road, clambering all over our vehicle. I was concerned they may get injured or hurt and as I could see them through the window of the meeting room, I excused myself and went outside to speak to them. Under my breath, I mumbled, 'Do they not have schools to go to, these kids?' and my interpreter overheard me and answered, 'Jordan – No they don't, actually.' This unexpected answer immediately stopped me in my tracks. My interpreter explained to me that the nearest school was thirty kilometres north of the village and as most of the families were very poor, with no vehicles or fixed accommodation, these children would likely never experience school as I knew it. Although I was never a star pupil and no lover of my own time in education, it made me really sad that something I took completely for granted was actually a privilege that simply couldn't be found in many parts of the world. In that very moment I made a pledge to myself that one day I would make it my mission to try and help children living in these countries access some form of basic schooling. I remember that moment like it was yesterday and the words of my interpreter will stay with me for ever…

Back on a patrol in mid-2005, we were heading to a police station in a place called Majar al-Kabir in southeastern Iraq. It was a place that had always been a hotbed of insurgent activity and was notorious for being the place where six Royal Military Police lost their lives two years earlier in 2003. The six RMPs were slaughtered in tragic circumstances which saw a routine patrol in the area spiral into a serious public order situation with an angry mob of up to 600 people taking on a small British military section. The troops on the ground were both seriously outnumbered and outgunned. The incident is still surrounded by political controversy as to what in fact really happened on that dark day.

I was attached to the Coldstream Guards on this particular day when we came across a group of children about three kilometres north of the town. We were en route to a meeting with the police commander in Majar al-Kabir at the very station our colleagues had been killed, and I was nervous and apprehensive as there had always been trouble in this place for one reason or another. As we approached the large group of kids, they appeared to be in distress and were shouting and screaming for help. I was peering through the hatch on the top of my Land Rover, holding my rifle steady to provide what we called 'top cover' for the patrol, and could see that something was not right here. A small Iraqi boy ran out into the middle of the narrow road to wave us down and I remember my first thoughts were, this is a trap or an ambush of some sort. I could hear Sergeant 'Jonah' Jones, my vehicle commander, also expressing similar thoughts to the other vehicle commanders. Consequently, we were all extremely cautious in our approach. The problem was, we couldn't avoid the child without going off road, but the road had a small stream running down either side, which ultimately made the decision for us that we had to stop. There was nothing else for us to do.

As we dismounted we could see that one of the children

had been seriously injured. He was suffering a catastrophic bleed from his right leg. He had inadvertently activated an improvised explosive device (IED), a bomb that would've likely been placed to take out our patrol, or perhaps another patrol passing through. It could have been lying there for days, or it may have been laid that morning especially to maim or kill us. The local police knew what time we were coming and corruption was rife in the Iraqi police force at this time, so it wasn't an alltogether ridiculous assumption to make that there may have been some collusion. We were never to know who planted it, but more importantly we had an innocent young boy to deal with who had triggered this device by accident, simply by going about his daily business playing along the roadside with his friends. We all carried tourniquets and military field dressings in our bottom-left trouser pockets, so I put my training into practice and patched the young boy up in a makeshift manner until the patrol team medic arrived on the scene a couple of minutes later from the rear vehicle. The boy was screaming and terrified and probably didn't know what was going on. His frightened screams alerted some local farmers who started to gather and once again there was the potential for the situation to spiral out of control quite quickly. Fortunately, a truck driver pulled over to provide us with assistance. He spoke some basic English and was able to explain to the locals what was going on. It's very easy to get tunnel vision in these situations as everyone wants to help and everyone wants to know and see what's going on, but as with any incident, the main priority has to be our own safety first. We were deep into enemy territory and there were only twelve of us on patrol, so we had to secure the area quickly and make sure there were no threats to our own lives before we started treating the casualty further and organising an extraction.

We wanted to take the boy back to camp to get him some proper medical treatment, but the locals would not allow this to happen. Jonah kindly offered to send a medic out from the camp on patrol later that day, but it was clear the people didn't want to be associated with British forces in any way. Having us coming around to their house would compromise their own security and they could be considered informants or agents for coalition troops. The insurgents and local militia didn't give second chances to those involved in assisting us. This was just one of the sad realities of war, and once again it was the children who were the innocent victims.

The innocents of war have always been there. They are not hidden from view, but stare at us right in the face. As a serving soldier, I couldn't help but think how fortunate I was to be able to eventually go home to a peaceful life without the worry of a bomb being dropped on my house at any moment, and how I could walk to the local shop to buy the daily newspaper without the fear of being shot. Most of us in the army at that time, young as we were, tried not to think too deeply about what we were witnessing because it was often too painful to comprehend. Instead, we were intent on cracking on with the job, getting that current tour over and done with and getting back home as quickly as possible. But I never forgot the devastation and guilt I felt about seeing how the children suffered. I carried it with me...

It was while serving in the British Army that I suffered a serious injury that put me out of the game completely. My back was seriously knackered – a double disc bulge and damaged cartilage and ligaments. Bang went my military career. I was frustrated, in pain and could no longer carry any heavy weights on my back from that moment onwards. Two years' worth of depressing and boring rehab at the military rehabilitation centre in Tidworth, with regular stints in Headley Court, followed.

God, it was dull. My days were spent swimming, stretching, jogging and learning to balance properly. My posture had always been appalling (I was a bit of a sloucher), so the rehab helped a little with that, even though my posture remains poor to this day. It was like being back at school again, and brought back a few memories of being bored out of my skull. I studied the biometrics of the human body and was taught how to walk and sit properly. It was the banter and camaraderie that got me through, so it wasn't a total dead loss. Everyone else at the centre seemed to be as bored and fed up as me, but somehow we managed to get ourselves and each other through it.

The final conclusion was that they couldn't fix me. But, the Catch-22 was that I was also too fit to be medically discharged. I could still do certain jobs within the military, but not combat or front-line soldiering. I didn't fancy doing a support role in the stores or in logistics. I'd joined the army to *be* a soldier, to carry the guns myself, not someone who gives out the guns *to* the soldiers.

It was during rehabilitation that the army came up trumps and offered to finance my study for a foundation degree. I grabbed at the chance, knowing that should I leave the army I needed to be equipped with the right tools and the right education. It was a dog-eat-dog world out there and I sure wasn't going to be chewed up and spat out.

It wasn't easy. A massive challenge, in fact, considering I'd bollocksed up everything at school. But I also knew I didn't want to be just another cog in the system, that I needed something to differentiate myself from the average ex-squaddie. If I wanted to work in security, I knew I'd be up against guys from Special Forces with incredible backgrounds. They would be my major competition and I would need to be up to the job, both physically and mentally. I had to pull something out of the bag, but I still didn't know exactly what that looked like. Cue massive relief when an old mate rang me up out of the blue and offered me security work on some oil and gas tankers out in the Middle East. The pressure was off, at least for a while.

My foundation degree was swiftly followed by an under-graduate and then a post-graduate degree in maritime security and risk management, all funded by the military. I was conscious of some of my mates in civvy street who had gone to university and had debts up to their eyeballs, so these offers of funding were a no-brainer really. I would say it was a lucky break, but then again I don't believe in luck. Lucky breaks are for the lazy and unprepared. I wasn't either of those, that was one thing I was sure of. Most of my studies were done in my cabin, head down while my mates were watching DVDs or hanging around. They ripped the piss out of me, but it was all done in good spirits. I'd get on that boat with an extra bag full of textbooks for the three-month voyage and just get on with it. I learned to be extraordinarily disciplined in the face of my mates' ribbing. The study bug had got me and I found I rather enjoyed the cut and thrust of academic debate. Critical thinking was a new set of skills to get my head round.

Somehow, I managed to pull the rabbit out of the hat and before long I got to be a specialist advisor on the economic impact of Somali-based piracy on global trade and how to mitigate against maritime cyber threats. I felt good, the world felt good. I was achieving great stuff, my parents were proud of me, I was hanging out with a great bunch of guys, using my brain, earning decent money and looking after those I loved. Good times were happening... until it all went tits up.

CHAPTER THREE

A BROKEN MAN

I was in the army when I first met Laura, still undergoing rehab and probably with another eighteenth months or so to go before I was back out on civvy street. I was still a young lad, with plenty to learn about life. Even though I had seen more than most civilians of the same age, I probably wasn't as grown-up in some areas as I should have been. Mind you, with hindsight, I was nothing like some of the regular knife-carrying crew around nowadays, intent on causing murderous havoc on Britain's city streets. Then, I simply hung around with my mates, drinking beers in the pub most weekends and chatting up girls to my heart's content. I certainly never did anyone any intentional damage.

A large group of us, maybe fifteen or so, coached up to a nightclub in Bath, Somerset. Laura was one of the women on the coach from Andover, the town I was living in near the army camp. I'd seen Laura walking and shopping around the town and had already noticed her, so when a mutual friend told me she was up for coming that night, I checked her out on Facebook to find photographs of her friends and family to try and get an early jump on her hobbies and likes. When I saw this gorgeous blonde sitting on the coach chatting happily to her friend, I was smitten all over again.

We arrived at Bath, leapt off the coach eager for the fun to start and all piled into this rather scabby-looking club. It was dark, the carpet was sticky, the music was pumping and there was a distinct whiff of urine and stale fags in the air. Not quite the atmosphere I was hoping for. Although I was quite drunk at the time, I remember being desperate to impress this gorgeous girl. She looked really fit, had a ton of energy and was obviously into all this healthy lifestyle stuff. When she told me she went to spin classes several times a week, I was like, 'Oh, yeah, I love spinning, I do it regularly myself actually.'

'Yeah... right,' she said.

So, there I was, busily spinning her a line about my military heroics as a dolphin trainer and my underwater knife-fighting skills, which was obviously a load of bullshit, when some equally drunk guy, holding a bottle of red wine in one hand and a glass of the stuff in the other, pushed right into me. The lot splashed down the front of my newly pressed white shirt like a scarlet gash.

'Oi, fucking arsehole, watch where you're going,' I yelled.

'Oh, piss off, mate,' he replied, shoving me hard. Bad move. I shoved him back even harder. On and on it went until a couple of bouncers clocked the commotion and tried to break it up.

Hauling me by the scruff of my jacket, someone very burly chucked me straight out the back door and told me to 'Get the fuck out of the club.' Fortunately, Laura decided to leave with me. So, off we went, just the two of us, giggling down the road and knocking drunkenly into lampposts. We ended up in another nightclub, a more salubrious one this time, with blue strobe lighting, leather banquettes and a menu of fancy cocktails propped up on the bar. I took Laura by the hand and pulled her onto the wooden dancefloor with me. After a couple of minutes of sweaty, slow dancing and a bit of un- dercover fumbling, I pulled her in closer and began to snog her face off like I was back at the school disco. I'm surprised nobody told us to 'get a room', because I think we were the only cringeworthy couple at it on the dancefloor that night.

We'd been given a meeting location back at the coach at 02.00 in the morning. Laura and I had been having far too much fun and lost track of time. We were late back to the coach and I was jogging along, giving her a piggyback. By this time most of the buttons had completely ripped from my shirt, my face was covered in pink lipstick and we were both totally wasted, if the truth be told. Laura had a hole in her tights and a shoe stuffed in each coat pocket. Everyone else on the coach had had an equally good time and were rather merry, cheering us on as we drunkenly clambered back onto the coach. The driver had a right face on and was obviously pissed off because he'd been waiting with that coach for ages and probably wanted to get back home to his wife and his nice warm bed. He tutted loudly and mumbled something about 'bloody drunken yobs', as he cranked the gear stick into first and bumpily set off back to Andover.

Clearly entranced by Laura, I allowed her to convince me to take a spinning class with her. That first session I nearly died. I was really going for it, trying to impress her, my legs pumping like mad as I raised my bum off the seat and leaned forward into the darkened studio and the beat of the music. All in all, I think I went to about seven spinning classes in two weeks. I've never done so much spinning in all my life. She obviously thought, 'Oh, a soldier, he'll love fitness.' Believe it or not, I've never loved fitness. It's never something I've been seriously into, even though I went on to make a big deal of it. I've never been the sort of person who jumps out of bed and can't wait to run, row or cycle. I have to really psych myself up for it, which is why I need challenges to rise to. Years later, Laura and I laughed our socks off at the thought of me trying to woo her with spinning dates. Seems like a lifetime ago now.

Six months after our first meeting and in a burst of manic passion, Laura and I got engaged. Three months after that, Laura was pregnant. It seemed ironic that I'd recently bought a really cool car – a brand new two-seater BMW convertible – and now I'd never get to enjoy the playboy lifestyle I thought I once craved. Although I didn't recognise it at the time, that little bump of belly grew to be worth far more to me than any cool sports car.

Initially we were living with Laura's parents in Andover because we were trying to save for a house of our own. Her mum and dad were kind to me, letting us stay in their neat and tidy suburban home for some considerable time, probably far longer than either of them enjoyed. Living in a small house was stressful for all of us, especially as I had a bad habit of leaving my kit lying around – body armour, helmets, all sorts of military stuff. It must have really got on their nerves. Respect to Laura's parents for letting me stay; it's not easy living right on top of other people and their mess. Although camouflage clothing is great for tactical operations, it certainly isn't complementary to the decor in most people's homes!

A few months later, much to the relief of Laura's mum and dad, we moved into our first home, which was also in Andover. We were so looking forward to starting life on our own terms and being independent, but sadly the honeymoon period didn't last long. Everything had happened so quickly in our lives together, the engagement, the pregnancy, the new house. Neither of us were prepared for having a child and especially one that came along so early in our relationship. We were both kids really and still getting to know each other properly. But our daughter's birth in Winchester hospital was the proudest day of my life and my greatest achievement. It's one thing that I'll never forget and one that I know will sustain me throughout my life. Holding little baby Evie in my arms just did it for me. I was full of love and grand dreams for the future, but the experience of fatherhood also brought back memories of the tragic lives of the children I had seen in Iraq, and something deep and unnameable in the back of my mind was brought alive.

I had a young family to support and my work in maritime security was on the upswing. My studies had paid off and I was now working away on the ships for months at a time in places like the Indian Ocean, the Gulf of Aden, the Straits of Malacca and the Red Sea. The downside was that Laura and I spent many months apart, so she had to be both Mum and Dad to Evie while I worked to pay for our new home. She was a great mother, one of the best in fact, but I simply wasn't there enough at the early stages to help out. I missed my girls when I was working, but I was very focused and driven. It was easy for me to take Laura for granted and rely on the fact that she was keeping it all together at home in the fortress, while I was out in the world, bringing in the money. In retrospect, I was naïve; I just thought I was doing my job. It's what I'd done since I was sixteen years old. Working away from home with limited communications was nothing new to me. I'd never found it necessary to keep in direct contact with a loved one day in and day out before. It was something I was used to, but it was much harder for Laura and I didn't fully appreciate that at the time.

Looking back, I admire her enormously for putting up with me being away so much. I'd be sure to take the load when I was back on shore to give Laura a rest, but when I was away I was on my own path, selfishly chasing my own dream and hoping it was a dream we both shared. I simply wanted to provide both Laura and Evie with the best I could give them. I thought I was doing the right and manly thing.

But, in reality, it wasn't the life Laura wanted, and who could blame her? She missed me and our life together as partners and parents to Evie. Laura gave me enough warnings, enough messages to let me know she was unhappy, but I didn't take them. 'I'm sick and tired of being ignored and left to do all the parenting by myself. I might as well be a single mum left to do all the grind by myself, 'cos you do bugger all. It's so easy for you swanning off whenever it all gets too much,' she said to me more than once.

Laura worked as a beauty therapist consultant, sometimes late into the evening. It was a lot of hassle for her to organise appropriate childcare for Evie. It resulted in plenty of friction between us when we tried to balance our bread-winning versus our parenting roles. She threatened to leave me countless times unless I changed my attitude and give her more time and attention. But I was intent on grabbing all those work opportunities with both hands as they came at me thick and fast. They wouldn't last for ever and I was managing to give us what I thought was a good life and pay all the bills at the same time. It was simply too much to walk away from and I couldn't do it. Life's opportunities are a bit like train carriages rolling by. There you are standing on the platform and the train passes by like life passes by. Opportunities come and go every day, but it's up to you to jump on that carriage and grab whatever's passing by on that train. The hardest thing is recognising those opportunities, and you either jump on board or let go. I knew I was a workaholic and it's something I tried to keep a lid on, but I loved what I did and often found it hard to differentiate work from pleasure.

Much to my distress, I found early fatherhood difficult and I'm not too proud to admit that I struggled. The advent of becoming a father and going away to sea was a dramatic combination of both burden and exhilaration. Every time I came home from a long absence, I would have to start building the relationship again with poor Evie. She would stare at me quietly for the first few days, clinging to her mum, unsure of who I was, or whether I was someone she could trust. She would look at me shyly, hiding her face in her mother's skirt, and it would take two or three days to coax her round and get her to relax with me before things got back to 'normal' again and Evie was back to her cheery self. It was difficult for me and Laura too. It's hard maintaining a relationship when one of you is away for two to three months at a time; you tend to get used to being away from each other. I hate that old adage, 'out of sight, out of mind', but sometimes it's true. Sadly, Laura ended up clearly resenting my work. 'You don't show me enough affection,' she said. 'You're in love with the job, not me. I understand you work away. I understand you're highly motivated and career-driven. All I ask is that when you're with me, you try to show me a bit more affection. Show me the love I need.'

I guess all she wanted was what every woman would want, just a bit of kindness, attention and TLC. I was probably too self-absorbed at that time to give her what she needed. In retrospect, this was definitely the hazy beginnings of my slowly unwinding relationship.

But I wasn't a total idiot. I always made sure I was there for the important milestones in Evie's life – birthdays, first steps, first day at school and the like – but it didn't cut the mustard with Laura. I don't blame her for feeling resentful, but neither do I think she really got the fact that it was all for her and Evie. Laura may have enjoyed all the good times, but she didn't seem to fully understand that it came with huge sacrifices too. Sadly, I think we were both in the wrong and were unable to find any middle ground where it mattered.

It got so tough and I got so fed up with the bad atmosphere that in the end I decided to quit working away from home altogether and start running my own business in the maritime security industry as an independent consultant. I knew the business like the back of my hand by now and I hoped running my own risk advisory company would allow me more time in the UK and subsequently more time with my family. But I was being sadly over-optimistic and probably unrealistic, because it didn't take long for me to find that running my own business came with its own pressures and ended up taking more of my time than working on the ships ever did. My mind was always on the bloody laptop or the phone, or where I was supposed to be and who I was supposed to be meeting. It was a never-ending cycle of work and pressure that took up all my time and brain space. Both Laura and Evie began to suffer even more from my emotional absence.

The eventual realisation that my relationship with Laura was crumbling sent me into a tailspin of severe depression and anxiety. I was fearful of the whole house of cards collapsing and losing both my girls. Laura and I embarked on a number of rescue strategies, including counselling and various therapies. All were helpful, but I think we both knew deep down inside that nothing was ever going to work. Although we carried on for the sake of our daughter, in the end it was Laura who drove the breakup. I simply didn't have the balls to do it; I couldn't!

When Evie was seven, Laura informed me that we were going to tell our daughter together that Mummy and Daddy were still Mummy and Daddy and always would be, that we still loved her a lot, but that we were not going to be living together any more. The plan was that I was going to lead the conversation.

The three of us were sitting squeezed up together on the small couch in the living room. Evie was between me and Laura; Laura was clutching a cushion on her lap; Evie was holding a stuffed toy. I was scratching my face with apprehension. Evie knew something was up at once because I was in so much emotional pain. I started to cry, the tears were streaming down my face. I couldn't talk, so Laura ended up having to take over and explain to Evie that her parents were separating. Evie had never seen me cry before and it frightened her. She couldn't take the emotional pressure and ran upstairs to her room. Laura and I followed quickly before she got the chance to shut herself in. The situation was so emotionally fraught and desperate that the three of us ended up seeking comfort in one big family cuddle. It will always be one of the saddest days of my life.

Looking back, our impending separation was probably the trigger for a long road of negative events. Although I was quite aware we were splitting up – that it was in fact actually happening – it was still very hard for me to accept. I think we all have an image of living in this perfect world where two kids, maybe a family pet and a mum and dad all live happily ever after. I was clinging on to the hope that we could sort it all out and eventually resolve the whole sorry mess. Laura tried hard to be headstrong and disciplined, while I completely wussed out, breaking down and asking to try again. The poor girl didn't even want to be with me, but I'd convince her to give it another go because the split was seriously affecting all of our lives.

Laura was still living with me in the same house, but we were living lonely and separate lives. She had her own bedroom and I had mine, but we were divided by more than a brick wall. Laura kept herself busy working long days. She dropped Evie off at school in the morning, but would often not finish work until ten or eleven o'clock at night. Because we were both working at that time, Evie would go to her nan's house and eat her dinner there. But as the black dog of depression loomed ever nearer and I could feel him practically scratching at my heels, I stopped accepting any maritime consultancy work. I couldn't face it and when work was offered, I simply lied and said I was too busy. I wasn't in the right frame of mind to think about work. In reality, I was sitting on my sofa finding comfort at the bottom of a glass of beer.

I came from a family that didn't drink much at all; my

parents would have a drink at family functions, or maybe a pint of beer or a glass of wine on the odd weekend and of course at Christmas, but they certainly didn't have the fridge stacked with booze ready to be consumed when needed. I did though, I was binge-drinking alone on a daily basis when Laura was out. My thoughts and feelings were out of control and anxiety was a constant and unwelcome presence.

Eventually, things got out of hand and I stopped getting out of bed at a decent hour, spending each morning lolling in my pit until almost noon. I stopped showering, I stopped shaving; in all honesty, I began to live like a total mess. I felt utterly deflated and didn't even have the energy to open the living room curtains. I just sat there on my own in the dark, feeling sorry for myself and necking warm beer straight from the can. To add to my misery, I punished myself further by getting involved in online gambling. I've always liked a bit of a flutter, but I soon found myself gambling on really stupid things like bloody badminton games in Japan; things that I didn't know or care anything about.

As the weeks went by and I began to bother less and less about cooking proper meals for myself, I noticed I was developing a paunch. Standing in front of the mirror it was obvious I was beginning to put weight on from all the beer calories. Eventually, I started to feel so self-conscious I began to hate socialising in case someone noticed my obvious laziness and distinct lack of discipline.

One evening I was at a mate's house with a false smile plastered across my face, pretending everything was fine in my world, when the very thing I dreaded happened. 'Bloody hell, Jordan, you've put on some timber!' a voice blurted out. I felt right sorry for myself and a little offended if the truth be known. But, then, how did my mate know what was going on behind the scenes in my tawdry life? I tried to laugh it off good-naturedly. Banter was a normal thing between me and my mates and I'm sure no offence was meant. But I slunk off home feeling thoroughly defeated and crawled into my lonely bed.

Then came a much-needed reality check. My mum was due to come round. The kitchen was a shit pit with old crushed beer cans lying around and piles of dirty dishes left on the side of the drainer. It looked like someone had been squatting there for weeks. 'Fucking hell,' I thought, 'I'm drinking way too much here.' I spent the next couple of hours cleaning like the devil before mum saw the mess and realised my life was spiralling out of control. The last thing I wanted was to worry her any more than I had to. I'd never hear the end of it.

Laura and Evie began to spend more and more time out of the house because of the awkwardness of the situation. We weren't together, but I was always pestering her to be together. I was a pain in the arse in many respects. It's not pleasant hanging around miserable people and Laura and I were arguing about the smallest and silliest of things like who parked in what space on the driveway, or me not putting the loo seat down after I'd had a pee. Our fights were escalating too. Whereas Laura used to say, 'Jordan, clean up your shit,' she now yelled, 'Are you fucking taking the piss…?' She didn't want her daughter living in this kind of environment and who could blame her? It wasn't exactly an appealing home to cosy up in any more. It looked more like a halfway house for deadbeats.

One day, Laura had to call an ambulance because my anxiety was debilitating and I was worrying the life out of her. The female paramedics came into my room where I was lying crippled in my bed. 'This is horrible. I've got something really wrong with me,' I cried. I was doubled up with some kind of crazy stomach pain, shitting all over the place and convinced I was seriously ill. My stomach was cramping so badly, I literally thought I was on my death bed at this point. The paramedics did a few tests on me, patted me motherly on the shoulder and told me to relax. I saw one of them turn to Laura and whisper, 'Is your relationship going through a tough time at the moment? Does Jordan have any problems in his life, any job or financial worries?'

'Yeah, we've got a lot of challenges at the moment,' replied Laura.

'Well, that's some serious build-up of acids and stomach cramps. He seems under a lot of stress. He's really got to do something about it. Try your best to get him to see his GP.'

I was embarrassed because the second female paramedic attending was an ex-military combat medic and I didn't want her to think I was a loser (and indirectly a failure as a man). She looked at me and quietly said, 'Come on, Jordan, you need to man up now. You're an ex-soldier.' She was trying to give me advice without offending me or Laura. She obviously knew from her experience what was up with me, but she didn't want to tell me because of my masculine pride or something. Thinking about it a few days later, I deciphered she was sort of saying, 'There's nothing wrong with you that's going to kill you, but you need to sort yourself out and take control.'

By this time, Laura and I both knew our relationship had gone beyond merely crumbling and that our way of dealing with it wasn't working, but somehow we'd both keep convincing each other we could make a go of it. We probably went on for about a year like that, damaging everyone in the process, including our wider families. The whole episode was a vicious cycle of psychological torture for everyone.

Eventually, Laura and I decided to live apart and I began to half-heartedly date other people. Laura went to New Zealand for a month or two to escape the on-going drama. She wanted to get away from me for some peace and quiet, a bit of fun and to get her head straight. It was a big move for her to leave Evie with me and her mum for so long, but she needed to for her own sake and I don't blame her.

Much to my shock, she met some guy out there and they

posted several pictures of themselves looking happy and 'together' on social media. I didn't truly understand the power of social media then, that we perceive and believe what we choose to perceive and believe, that what we see is not what is necessarily happening. When I got wind of it, I made a big fuss and was madly jealous. I tortured myself, convinced I wanted her back, even though the relationship was well over.

Soon after this, I met a lovely woman who was very good to me, but I didn't treat her at all well. All the time I was seeing this other woman I was still secretly trying to get Laura back because I was so jealous of her being with another man. I wasn't in control of myself or my life and I was playing a very dangerous game. My emotions were all over the place. Although I looked calm on the surface, I was in turmoil. Like a duck, my legs were paddling furiously below the waterline. I showed a complete lack of respect for both women.

When Laura returned from New Zealand it soon became obvious she was going out on regular dates with other guys. There were late nights and pretty dresses, more make-up than usual and far more smiles on her face. In a way I was happy not to have a headache about my work. Laura wasn't there to nag me and I could just get on with my life and my work without being made to feel bad about it. I guess I was just surviving at that point and trying not to think too hard about what it all meant, but it was a bloody awful time.

One day, too fearful to face me and frightened of my

reaction, Laura sent me a text: 'I have to tell you something and you might not like it and it will probably hurt you, but I've truly moved on. I've met someone, it isn't a fling, it's somebody I really like and he likes me and we want our relationship to go public. I don't want you to hear about it through the grapevine, I want you to hear it from me. I don't want to have to walk around on eggshells, worried we might bump into you on a night out.'

Fair play, but the whole thing was really weird and I found it extremely hard to accept. I hate failure and I was still trying to cling on to the idea of a happy family. I didn't want to be with Laura, but I didn't want anyone else to have her either. I wanted her to remain all mine, which was clearly not a helpful position for either of us.

I soon found myself in the funk of the deadliest depression, but I tried not to blame others for my mess. Somewhere in the back of my mind I knew I was the only one who could take responsibility for crawling out. Laura and I had known each other for almost ten years by this point and I was well aware I had a responsibility to both her and Evie. In the end we acted like adults, shook hands and pledged to do the best for our daughter. We finally divided up our assets formally and I attempted to move on.

CHAPTER FOUR

THE BLACK DOG

My attempt at moving on was a fool's errand. I'd always thought depression and anxiety was some bullshit thing people made up when they were feeling a bit down or wanted a duvet day from work. It hit me like a four-ton truck and I was in total denial. There was no way a big strong guy like me was going whimpering to some doctor. I was six foot two inches, sixteen stone, fought pirates for a living, knew how to handle a gun and thought of myself as a bit of a tough guy. I couldn't face the humiliation. I couldn't get my head round losing who I thought was my partner for life. I felt like a fraud, a loser, and some days I simply felt numb, with no feeling whatsoever. Most of the time I felt like a big black cloud was following me everywhere, just hovering above my head ready to engulf me. If anyone tried to do something nice for me, I would wonder, 'What's the catch?' Nothing made me happy

and I had a constant feeling of underlying dread. It was suffo-
cating and frightening.

The dreadful anxiety was like a snowball; once it started
rolling downhill, it was almost impossible to stop. Body
awareness, breathing and knowing my symptoms were only
one side of the coin. The other was actually changing my anxious behaviour, which in the moment was extremely difficult
to do because the momentum was so powerful. Whatever
was driving my anxious behaviour felt urgent and dire. Often,
anxiety isn't really about what we are anxious about. For me,
it was the fear of failure, of rejection, of not feeling good
enough. The fact I had no urge to be productive bugged me.
I felt scared and tired at the same time. I wanted friends, but
hating socialising. I wanted to be alone, but didn't want to be
lonely. I cared about everything, then cared about nothing. I
felt everything at once, then felt paralysingly numb.

I was still managing to just about adequately function in
my role as a professional security consultant, until the day
it all got beyond me and I found myself up on that roof in
Dubai. As I paced backwards and forwards contemplating
a leap towards oblivion, my phone buzzed, startling me and
bringing me back to the present. It was a text from Mum
asking if I was OK. Call it a mother's sixth sense, but she
knew something was up. Seeing her text triggered more serious emotions. All the good things we had shared as a family

started running through my mind and I did what most young men do when they feel their world evaporating… I phoned my mum. I thought, do I want to tell my mum where I am and what I'm doing or will it freak her out? She wasn't totally aware of my miserable mental state – no one was to be honest, I hid it all very well, I'd almost become a professional at it – but she heard enough in my voice to know I was in trouble. 'What's up, Jord?' she asked, 'You don't sound right. Are you having a tough time, love?'

'Laura's met someone else. She sent me a text to say that she's moved on and I've seen it all over social media.'

'She's young Jordan, just having fun,' Mum said. 'You know what it's like, I'm sure it means nothing, just some random guy. Don't get upset, you're not together any more anyway, remember. It's time to let go now, it really is.'

My lovely mum was, and still is, one of those annoyingly level-headed people who never takes sides, but if she has to, it's always for a moral or ethical reason. She quite often took Laura's side if she didn't agree with my attitude or behaviour, whereas Laura's mum always took her side, no matter whose fault it was.

'Don't do anything stupid, Jord. Think of Evie,' she said. 'She needs her father. I just spoke to her yesterday. She's doing well at school, you know. She had a starring role in her school play and she really misses you.'

In hindsight, it was clear Mum was being really clever here and using a bit of emotional blackmail to rein me in. Me, I was just thinking about all the shit going on in my life. I was concentrating on building up all the drama and the stress of the relationship breakdown and making a massive deal of it all. I wasn't thinking about the fact I had a beautiful, healthy daughter. There was no space for anything positive because my mind was a pressure cooker about to go off. Mum was planting little bite-sized chunks of positivity to bring the emotional seesaw level again.

Mum's new narrative made me start to question myself. In retrospect I understood why people think about topping themselves. Extreme levels of stress and pressure are blinding. They smother you, then rub out all the good feelings and replace them with a mixture of numbness and pain. I thought about the many friends and colleagues I'd lost in places like Iraq and Afghanistan. I thought about everything I'd endured and witnessed in various war zones with the King's Royal Hussars, all the horrors I'd seen and the desperate lives of the children. Thinking of the innocents who suffered the most and their desperate experiences cut me to my core. I wondered how much of that I had been a part of. I thought about how very lucky I was to still be here alive and able to feel something, even if those feelings were painful. I had to acknowledge to myself that, unlike many others, I was immensely fortunate to have problems that could actually be solved one day and that I was still in a position to fix them. I was, after all, still above the ground and not yet below it. 'Fuck it, Jordan,' I said to myself, 'you're still here and that's a lot luckier than most people who would give their right arm to take one more breath on this planet.' I'd had enough of being in denial and blaming my troubles on others.

With Mum's words ringing in my ears, I did a full U-turn, thinking what a sick bastard I must be to even consider jumping into oblivion when there are good men and women who will never see their partners and kids again. I realised I was being selfish, wrapped up in my own troubles, and that my daughter needed me. She needed a good dad, a good role model in life. My taking the 'easy way out' wouldn't help her at all. I had no right to dump her in the fatherless club. That would be the equivalent of spitting on the values I so lauded. Soldiering had been a high-stakes game, a literal game of life and death, and here I was snivelling to myself on a rooftop in Dubai.

When I returned home to the UK after the drama of Dubai, still feeling emotionally fraught, I went to visit Laura to talk about one of Evie's upcoming school functions which I wanted to attend. Laura and I were sitting quite companionably together at her kitchen table and drinking tea when she turned to me and stroked my hand. 'You look dreadful, Jord.

You're obviously not looking after yourself properly. You can't carry on like this,' she said. 'You're a danger to yourself and you're making life miserable for the rest of us.'

I put my head in my hands, worried I was frightening Laura. 'Come on, we'll get some help. Try and sort this out together,' she said. First stop was a local NHS doctor. I didn't really want to go. I didn't want to have to explain myself to a stranger, no matter it was a doctor. I was in a foul mood all the way to the surgery and had a face on like a bad smell. After waiting for forty minutes in the waiting room and getting more and more anxious, I was eventually allowed in to see the doc. I explained my symptoms and how I was feeling. 'Classic signs of PTSD, Mr Wylie,' he replied. But I knew this wasn't PTSD. I knew what PTSD looked like, smelled like and felt like. I'd seen it many times in guys who I'd served on combat operations with.

'No, this isn't PTSD, this is something else,' I said.

'Ah, but I think you're probably denying the truth here, Mr Wylie,' the doc replied.

'No, I've come to terms with everything I've seen, all the limbs shattered, all the bodies I've seen blown up,' I insisted. 'In fact, I consider it an absolute honour to talk about it and keep the flag flying in memory of all those we've lost.'

For many people and lots of my former colleagues, remembering friends killed in service brings up horrific memories. Personally, I always try to keep things positive and keep the happy memories of things shared, alive and vibrant. So, to be suddenly side-swiped into a pit of depression and negativity really agitated me.

Nowadays I look at every day as a gift because I don't know which day might be my last. I'm not fearful of dying, and although it might look like it at times from my expeditions and extreme adventures, I'm certainly not reckless with my life. I believe that everyone has an expiry date and when your time's up, it's up, whether that be fighting in a war zone, running in a conflict region, driving down the road, or just cooking in your kitchen. I'm not a particularly religious man, but when I was in a combat zone, I always carried the military Bible that was given to me on day one of military training by Padre David Barratt, a fellow Blackpool man. I told him I didn't really believe in God, but we used to joke together about both believing in the 'Tangerine Army', the nickname for our beloved Blackpool Football Club. I never actually read that Bible, but I did carry it with me. Call it superstition, or the eerie possibility of a higher power. Sometimes I like to think there is something out there, but I don't get caught up in it.

All in all, I had some pretty intense debates with the NHS doctors arguing my case against having PTSD. 'I recognise I'm not well. I understand I have psychological scars,' I said, 'but what I'm not recognising is that it's a result of combat, conflict and war... It's because I'm losing my fucking family, as well as my wits!'

'Don't worry, Mr Wylie, this denial is all part of the process, you just need to come to terms with everything you've seen and experienced in your tours of Iraq,' the doc replied. I felt like I was banging my head against a brick wall. Nobody was listening to me!

'I'm here because my daughter, who I love more than anything in the world and who is my greatest achievement and my proudest moment, is going to be living with another guy and I'm sorry, but I just can't get my head around that.'

In the end, I got so caught up in denying I was in denial, I became paranoid about the whole thing and then seriously had to question whether I was protesting too much and was in denial after all!

I hate the term 'Post-Traumatic Stress Disorder'. What's with the 'disorder' bit? It's not a disorder. Why not just call it post-traumatic stress? Drop the 'D' in PTSD. It's simply a natural reaction to an unnatural set of circumstances and nobody should feel sidelined or 'othered' by having it. It's far too easy for doctors to assume that just because you've been active in a war zone, got blown up a few times and seen your mates killed, that you're suffering from PTSD. Medical professionals do an amazing job, but sometimes they misdiagnose and stick a patient with psychological issues into the easiest bracket. Most people suffer from depression or anxiety at some time in their lives. It's just that some people are able to manage it better than others. We are all wired differently and respond to different things in different ways. There is no right or wrong, there is just different.

I wasn't doubting that PTSD exists. I know it does for sure; I've seen first-hand evidence. I was just doubting that I had it. The following is a story I came across doing the rounds on social media, sent to me by a friend who was also suffering from depression. It wasn't originally written by him, but I think it perfectly sums up the soldier's take on PTSD, so I say again – I hate the 'D' in PTSD. Post-traumatic stress is a perfectly normal reaction to extremely abnormal situations – let's drop the 'D', it's not a disorder!

A soldier who had been diagnosed with PTSD fell into a giant hole and was unable to get out. When an SNCO walked by, the soldier called out for help, but the SNCO shouted, 'Just get on with it, dig deeper and come through,' then he chucked him a spade. The soldier did as the SNCO told him and got on with digging that hole even deeper. A senior officer went by and the soldier called out for help again. The officer told him, 'Use the tools your SNCO has given you', then threw him a bucket. The soldier used the tools and dug the hole deeper still, until he eventually filled the bucket.

A psychiatrist walked by. The soldier called, 'Help me! I'm stuck here and I can't get out!' so the psychiatrist gave him some drugs and said, 'Take these. They will relieve the pain and you will forget all about the big old hole.' The soldier thanked him and followed his advice, but when the pills ran out he was still stuck in the hole.

A well-known psychologist then ambled by and heard the soldier's cries for help. He stopped and asked, 'How did you get there? Were you born there? Did your parents put you there? Tell me about yourself, it will alleviate your sense of loneliness.' So the soldier talked with him for an hour, then the psychologist told the soldier his time was up but he promised to be back next week. The soldier thanked him, but he was still stuck in the hole.

Another soldier, just like him, happened to be passing by. The soldier with PTSD cried out, 'Hey, help me. I'm stuck in this great big hole!' Right away the other soldier jumped down in there with him. The soldier with PTSD started to panic and said, 'What are you doing? Now we're both stuck down here!' But the other soldier just smiled and replied, 'It's OK, calm down, brother. I've been here before... I know how to get out.'

In the end, I was diagnosed with severe depression and chronic anxiety and left that doctor's consultation room clutching a prescription for an anti-depressant called Sertraline. 100 milligrams a day. I wasn't happy; I'd always been one of those people who didn't believe in taking a pill, thinking they were an admission of failure. I never even took painkillers for my very serious and career-ending back injury in the army. I was sceptical, but I did as the doctors told me and took the damn pills.

After two or three weeks I was thinking, 'I don't feel any different. What a load of horseshit. I'll just keep taking the drugs to keep everyone happy and limit any grief.' I didn't like the pharmaceutical market; I felt it forced a lot of people into addiction and over-reliance. I hated the idea of my system becoming inured to the meds and building up a tolerance. I didn't want to become one of those people who were ploughing them into their system month after month. But, as they became part of my day-to-day routine I understood it was more like putting fuel in your car or oil in your engine. I needed the pills to keep going and push on forward. My engine would still work without the right oil or petrol but it would work in a very rickety way. Once I put the lubricants in, after a few weeks everything started to work smoothly. But as much as I started to appreciate and benefit from them, the thought that I was becoming reliant on these drugs that I didn't want to be taking for the rest of my life churned away at the back of my mind.

The pharmaceutical market is a commercial operation and it's in the interests of all those companies to keep people on drugs; they make the world go round, and make a lot of people a lot of money. I'm not a big advocate of drugs, but I recognise they helped take me out of a very dark place and I feel no shame in needing them.

Even though Laura and I were no longer together as a couple, she was still very supportive on the mental health side. She would always check in on me and when I asked her why she bothered, she said, 'Because you're still a big part of my life. We have a child together. I want to make sure you're all right. What affects you, affects our daughter.' Every day she would text me to make sure I'd taken my tablets. She is a good woman without a doubt and I will always respect her – even if we don't always see eye to eye.

I also embarked on several courses of therapy, including cognitive behavioural therapy with an NHS counsellor, who again seemed intent on trying to drill my military experiences as the reason for my depression. I felt I was being pigeonholed once again into the PTSD bracket. All the therapist ever wanted to talk about was what I'd experienced in the military. It was never, 'Let's talk about not seeing your daughter', or 'Let's talk about the relationship breakdown', or even the financial pressures to pay the bills in a house I could no longer afford. Eventually, I got so sick of it I walked out halfway through session number three of five and went to see a private therapist. But I wasn't too keen when she gave me homework to do. I thought, 'Bloody hell, I've got enough work to do. I haven't the mental capacity or emotional energy to take on any extra.' I had to go home and write essays on my thoughts and feelings, while at the same time trying to find the time to get on with my normal job too. Paying a load of money out to a shrink in return for homework wasn't for me. It felt too much like high school.

I was blaming others for everything, not willing to take responsibility for my own actions, justifying myself and my behaviour until the cows came home. Moping around the house with Evie when she came to visit was beginning to take its toll on both of us. Sooner or later, I needed to get to the point where I actively accepted it was time to turn my life around, or I would lose Evie's respect and possibly her love too. My worry was that Laura might have given Evie a tainted opinion of me, although I had no reason to think she would. Laura wasn't one for bad-mouthing me in front of Evie. It was an unsubstantiated worry, but daughters judge their future encounters with men against the standards of their fathers and I hadn't always shown her my best side. I wanted to lead by example and needed to work damn hard to gain my daughter's esteem. My love for her was the major catalyst for the change I made in my life mentally and physically. I had a lot still going for me; I hadn't crashed out of life entirely. My personal life might have been utter shite but my professional life was going great guns. I had a lot to be grateful for and was a real believer in working hard to make positive changes. Acceptance is tough, but time is a great healer, if also a great cliché.

One day I went to a school summer fete on my own to see Evie dancing in a show. I knew Laura was going too and when I saw her there with her new boyfriend's arm around her, I realised that, quite miraculously, this no longer affected me.

'This is a game changer,' I thought, 'This is all right – this is a good thing to see. I feel OK about it.'

Laura's mum, Sharon, was walking around separately at the same village fete. Her mum had remained friendly and polite to me after the split, but then I felt she went and made things difficult by coming straight up to me and saying something I thought wasn't particularly helpful. She looked over at Laura and her new boyfriend, who were sitting loved-up together on a bale of hay and said, 'That could have been you, Jordan, couldn't it?' I think she was bitter that we'd all invested ten years of our lives in this relationship and in the end it didn't work out. I'm not sure it was an actual dig at me. Maybe she secretly hoped it really could have been me. Happy families and all that.

'You know what, Sharon,' I said, 'I don't know who this guy is, but seeing Laura that happy makes me happy.' I was genuinely delighted to see Laura smiling and looking happy again after so many years with me. I hadn't seen an honest smile on her face for such a long time. She's a great mum. I respect her and wish her all the best in life with her new partner. Thankfully, this isn't difficult for me to say any more.

Although the family breakdown was a terribly difficult time for all of us, looking back I believe it was all handled as best as it possibly could have been given the emotions involved, the issue of our daughter and the fact we shared property together. Both Laura and I certainly learned a lot about ourselves and ultimately we agreed to do our very best for our daughter. We both knew that even though it probably wasn't to be any more and although I had many regrets about decisions I'd made and perhaps the way I'd conducted myself at times, there were never any regrets (at least not from me) about getting together. We had created this beautiful miracle together who would always and forever be our beloved daughter. In order for me to patch things up and get back on track, I had to push my own troubles to one side, man up, so to speak, and get on with embracing life again. I'm sure Laura probably thought the same too. I guess Evie was the bridge of peace in the end.

It gets easier by the day. I love being an active dad. Evie has her own room at my house and Laura and I get on well, co-parenting our beautiful daughter. One of Evie's proudest moments is 'show and tell' day at school when she takes in a load of sweets and photos from my adventures around the world to share with her friends. She's quite adventurous herself now and very resilient. Chip off the old block.

CHAPTER FIVE

QUARANTINED

At this point, I was just busy trying to keep myself busy. Work was a soothing balm and gave me something else to think of other than my feelings of failure as a partner, which still occasionally reared their ugly head. I did have low points and was trying to stay positive, even though things had definitely turned a corner. Fortunately, my work had really picked up and I soon found myself engaged in an expedition with the American TV channel HBO, for two weeks. At the time I was still working as a consultant in maritime security and acting as the guide escorting a crew of about eight guys filming in the Gulf of Aden and the Horn of Africa. They wanted to get a better understanding of pirate activity in hostile environments and I was privileged to be asked to help them.

While showing the crew around one of the ports in the area I got bitten by a mosquito (actually, it was more like a battalion of the little bastards!). I thought nothing of it and carried on regardless. I was in Africa, after all, and being eaten alive by mozzies came with the territory, so it wasn't uncommon. But three days later it hit me hard. I was sick as a dog; my muscles were on fire and all I wanted to do was lie down. All the crew took the piss out of me, 'Ah, look at Jord, he can't take it, he's seasick.' I can't say I blame them for taking the mick out of me because I'd spent the past few days teasing them for getting so seasick themselves. The main presenter from the TV channel couldn't even operate because he was vomiting everywhere and I'd been laughing and joking with him, telling him to get a bloody grip of himself. As soon as I started to get sick myself, he gave it right back to me. But I'd been at sea for the past six years and knew this wasn't simply seasickness. I knew my own body and what seasickness felt like. This was something else, it felt really abnormal, too.

By the time I got back to the airport at Djibouti a few days later, I could hardly walk. My legs were all weak and wobbly and my muscles had turned to jelly. I had no control over my movements at all. My legs buckled beneath me and I fell flat on my face right there on the airport floor, banging my head hard as I fell. I had no idea what was happening to me. I was dripping with sweat, horribly nauseous, drowsy and had a thumping headache right behind my eyes. I just wanted to curl up and drift off somewhere quiet and dark. One of the film crew saw the state I was in and immediately phoned the emergency services. The next thing I knew I was in hospital in Djibouti with a massive needle stuck in my arm.

Ebola was running rampant at the time, and, being extremely contagious, was spreading like wildfire in Africa. So they stuck me on an Ebola ward in quarantine just to be on the safe side. Not surprisingly, nobody wanted to come near me because Ebola was spread by touch. Not knowing if I had Ebola or not, or whether I was going to live or die, frightened me and everyone else. The news had been full of 'Ebola, Ebola, Ebola', so naturally I thought, 'Shit, is this it? Is this the end?' I was stuck there in that room, all alone and waiting for a doctor to come along and give me news or information about my condition.

Ebola, a haemorrhagic fever of humans and other primates, is caused by a virus. The signs and symptoms (which typically start between two days and three weeks after contracting the virus) include a fever, sore throat, muscle pain and headache, and are swiftly followed by vomiting, diarrhoea and a rash with decreased function of the liver and kidneys. Horribly, at this stage, some people begin to bleed both internally and externally. The disease has a high risk of death, killing between 25 and 90 per cent of those infected, with an average of about 50 per cent. This is often due to low blood pressure from fluid loss and typically follows six to sixteen days after the first symptoms appear. I have always stated that dying is not something that really worries me or scares me, but the thought of having contracted Ebola absolutely floored me.

Ebola was mostly concentrated in West Africa. Even though I was now in East Africa, the medics knew I had been travelling around sub-Saharan Africa and were rightly concerned I'd picked it up and was now in danger of infecting everyone in Djibouti. My bed was covered with a white tent and I could see medics walking past dressed in what looked like white spacesuits. I was scared witless, so when the blood test results eventually came back with dengue fever and not Ebola, I was immensely relieved, but I still had a very high fever, a headache so fierce I thought my eyeballs were going to explode, and swollen lymph glands which made my face look like a chipmunk. Plus, my skin was peppered with a pink rash and my gums were sore and bloody. It wasn't a great look – I certainly wasn't going to be updating my Instagram for a while!

I knew my facts about dengue and was aware that millions of patients are hospitalised each year, but most people recover after two to seven days. Some, like me, are unfortunate enough to develop dengue haemorrhagic fever after the initial fever declines. This is a more severe form of the illness and can in some cases cause organ damage, severe bleeding, dehydration and – if you're super-unlucky – death.

I couldn't wait to get out of that hospital and back to the

QUARANTINED

UK. After three weeks of deathly quarantine in the hospital, I flew back, still feeling sick as a pig. As I waited for my bags to arrive at the carousel, my legs once again buckled from beneath me. I managed to get myself to the toilet where I unceremoniously threw up, desperate to get home and back into my own bed.

As I struggled through arrivals, lugging my bags behind me, I saw Keith, my regular taxi driver, waiting. Keith knew all my secrets. For the past ten years he had picked me up at various airports when I returned from overseas missions and various expeditions and adventures. He was the one who got his ear bent from me venting all my shit because he was quite simply the first bloke I talked to properly when my feet landed back on Blighty soil.

He shook my hand, took my bag from me, looked me straight in the eye and said, 'Jord, mate, you aren't looking too well, you look like you just done ten rounds with Mike Tyson!' Keith was always a great one for talking; he could chat the hind legs off a donkey. I had to tell him to shut up and leave me alone because I felt too ill to listen.

'Got it,' he said. 'Just don't be bloody sick in my taxi and tell me if you need to pull over.'

We found the car parked on the top floor of the arrivals parking lot at London Heathrow and I clambered into the back seat, anxious to lie down and close my eyes. As we drove down the M3 from London Heathrow to Andover, I knew

63

I was going to chuck. I tapped Keith hard on the shoulder, making a kind of gurgling noise. He pulled over onto the hard shoulder, where I got out of the taxi as quick as I could, bent over and spewed my guts onto the grass verge. Cars honked at me in solidarity as they sped on by regardless. I got back in the taxi to clean myself up and Keith handed me a packet of mints, extra-strong ones. 'Get them down ya,' he said.

After another ten minutes I felt my gorge rise again. 'Gotta stop, gonna puke,' I yelped, vomiting yellow bile.

'You've got to go to hospital, mate, there's definitely something wrong with you.'

'Nah, it's OK, I can make it home.'

'We've only done forty miles, and you've puked two times, already,' replied Keith. 'I'm taking you straight to the hospital, no arguments.'

So that's how I ended up in Winchester Hospital. I had all these records in French and broken English that the Djiboutians had given me. I handed them over, telling the medics I had dengue. I still felt really sick and once again I was placed in quarantine. Because I'd travelled from Africa they wanted to verify that it was indeed dengue and not Ebola, so I was put in an area away from all the other patients in my own private room where they did a barrage of tests.

There was no relief – I was still suffering badly from the backlash of the illness. I was hooked up to a drip and stayed curled up in the foetal position in chronic pain for a full

four-and-a-half days. I didn't tell my parents where I was because my mum is the biggest worrier in the world. I tend to
play things down when I'm around her. I think the second
time I went to Iraq, I didn't even tell her I was going, I just
went. I didn't text my next of kin, who was still listed as Laura
on my medical records even though we were no longer together, or anyone else for that matter. So I knew that if I told
them how unwell I was, they'd all be rushing down to see me,
and I was in no fit state to talk to anyone. I couldn't string a
sentence together. I felt so ill. I didn't even have the energy to
get my phone out; I simply wanted to close my eyes and lie
silently and uninterrupted in a darkened room.

Eventually, my symptoms abated. I stopped with the shiv-
ers and shakes and the nausea, and felt my body slowly re-set.
Home had never felt so welcoming. I might have survived
dengue and thought I was on a home run, but little did I know
the illness would have a serious impact on my health later
down the line – which had the potential to entirely scupper
my best-laid plans for the future. They say you never know
what's around the corner, and I sure as hell had no idea what
was to come…

CHAPTER SIX

A GROWTH MINDSET

The slow climb out of the pit of depression began with the final and long-awaited acceptance of the end of my relationship with Laura. I call this time the beginning of my post-traumatic growth. I was grateful for my health post-dengue fever; I'd made a full recovery. I was grateful for my profession, my friends, colleagues and my family. I was grateful, too, for the values instilled in me through my military service. One of those values, selfless commitment, or putting the needs of others before your own, was my guiding principle in the days and months to follow. I've always believed that if you can make a difference to improve other peoples' lives, then you absolutely should do so – no matter who you are or where you are. All of us, every single one of us, can make a difference in this world, however small, and I truly believe this from the bottom of my heart.

I was grateful for all the advantages and all the opportunities thrust at me throughout my life. My schooling and education, my three meals a day, my loving and stable parents, my access to clean drinking water, my safety. For many, experiencing trauma and pain helps them grow as people, although, understandably, most fail to see that in a crisis. With forethought, courage and planning, that pain can be put to good use. I spent a lot of time in reflection and with my new-found appreciation for life, I decided to change my mindset and forge ahead with a new and exciting project. My stumbling blocks had become stepping stones and I was keen to push a few boundaries, move forward and challenge myself. I knew I had a lot in me, a lot to give, and I was anxious to get back in the driving seat. I began to see my past failures as opportunities to do things differently. It's too easy to be a winner, to hold up the trophy and say, 'Look at me, look what I did. Aren't I clever?' It's far harder to learn new lessons by making mistakes. But those lessons are hugely valuable and stand the test of time exactly because they've been learned the hard way. When you've hit the low points too often, the highs seem glorious and you appreciate them even more.

Being in war zones and conflict zones and seeing first-hand all the challenges faced by the local population made me appreciate my own good fortune. Growing up on a pretty rough council estate in Blackpool is a walk in the park in comparison to those people struggling to survive in a war zone. But soldiering brings with it a host of other problems and in my opinion not enough care goes into post-traumatic growth. I've always found it fascinating that you can be fighting on the battlefield one day and on rest and recuperation the next, with no decompression period. I remember an incident where we were shooting at an enemy force with an exchange of fire in Iraq and fifteen hours later I was on a dance floor in Blackpool. It can be psychologically dangerous to take a guy from heavy combat where he's trained to kill to chatting up girls in the local pub or nightclub. You're having a pint, you're drinking shots and getting drunk, but there's no middle ground, which can be dangerous. It can't be good for your mental health, and as unbothered as you may be at the time because you're just so happy to be at home, I'm sure there are long-term effects. I've read plenty of stories in the news: 'Soldier Has a Fight on a Night Out', and he's up in court the next day for GBH, or ABH, or some assault charge and you just think, 'Who's that bloody idiot?'

But, in reality, how can you expect to take someone out of a combat zone where you're asking them to kill someone for their country, and then put them in a nightclub and give them excessive amounts of alcohol while they are still pumped full of testosterone. Twenty-four hours earlier, they were ready to kill someone! It's obvious how that just exacerbates the situation when somebody looks at them the wrong way, or spills a drink on them, or they chat up someone else's girlfriend. Training someone to be a killer one minute and then expecting them to be a pussycat the next is taking the piss. In my opinion, not enough care goes into looking after soldiers returning from combat operations and the government have wild expectations of returning military personnel. Many are just left to get on with it, which only causes more problems further down the line. Some are even prosecuted many years later for actions taken in conflict zones, with the case of Brian Wood MC, former Colour Sergeant, Princess of Wales's Royal Regiment, who was investigated by the Iraq Historic Allegations Team after being falsely accused of war crimes in Iraq, being a prime example. There are also many other ongoing cases where veterans of Operation Banner, the Northern Ireland conflict, are now being investigated for incidents from thirty to forty years ago. I can't even remember what happened in my life last week, never mind over a quarter of a century ago. It's an absolute tragedy that people are more concerned with causing our own troops problems in life than helping them adapt to civvy street. It really makes my blood boil.

I remember coming home halfway through a tour of the Middle East and I think five or six of us serving soldiers walked into the first bar we came to and the bouncer said, 'No, not tonight, lads.' All of a sudden we're thinking, 'What the fuck have we done wrong? We're fucking serving our country here and you're stood there with your doorman's badge on, gobbing off, telling us we can't even come in and have a drink.' Straight away your night starts out on a bum note, so someone lumps the doorman because just a few hours earlier, they were fighting for their lives in a war zone.

I didn't want to be that angry man who lumped strangers. I'd seen far too much anger running amok in conflict zones and knew how damaging this could be to one's own psyche, as well as to other people. It would be so easy to fall into that cliché of traumatised and angry former soldier. But I wanted – and needed – to grow. If post-conflict care from the authorities was thin on the ground then I would have to do it for myself. I knew three things now: that I didn't want to spend my life with a chip on my shoulder, that I wanted to help children gain access to education in war zones and that I had a passion for travel and adventure. I was ready to combine these two last things as the foundation for my future growth. The army had given me a thirst for discovery and adventure. When I was working on board vessels in the maritime security industry, I was sailing on some of the most dangerous seas, but when I was on land waiting between security jobs, I was lucky to appreciate some of the most beautiful places in the world like Mauritius, the Seychelles, the Maldives and Dubai.

All these exotic places were on the edges of the piracy areas I was working in, but they weren't places I truly wanted to explore. I was far more interested in scoping out new cultures, experiencing new food, new people and customs. Lying on white sand with a cocktail in my hand didn't really cut it for me. I was more interested in people's personal journeys, their stories and narratives and the way they made sense of the world and the human condition.

Ideally, I was looking for adventure somewhere off the beaten track. I wanted to escape the ordinary – as well as my own mind. I was desperate to go somewhere where there was no WiFi, no Starbucks and certainly no golden arches of McDonald's. I needed to help others who were at the mercy of violence at a time when I myself felt at my emptiest and weakest. Whether that choice was to self-soothe or because I had a genuine yearning to help those less fortunate was yet to be seen. A hundred different ideas floated through my mind, but I couldn't consolidate any of them. Eventually, inspired by the lives of the innocents that I'd seen first-hand while serving in Iraq, I decided to run for charity. I needed a reason to go back to the countries I had visited or served in, but this time in a capacity that could help people. As a soldier, I thought I was helping people to free themselves from insurgency and violence, but this thought is not always shared by the people you are supposedly fighting for. Many of the locals considered us invaders as we turned up in their countries with our guns and good intentions. Not everyone valued our presence. This time I wanted to see these countries from a different perspective. I also needed focus and purpose in my own life, so the idea for a project I was to call Running Dangerously wasn't completely altruistic. I was helping myself at the same time.

This expedition was about more than just raising money and awareness for various charities working with children in war zones, it was also about challenging the narrative and perceptions that people might have of these countries when they watch the news, read the paper or follow social media. Having spent most of my life as a soldier in conflict zones and in hostile environments, one of the things that affected me the most was the stories of the people I met – and more so than anything else – the tragic plight of the children. Watching the children deal with chaotic lives was horrific in many respects, but access to education could be a way out, an escape route to a safer, more prosperous life, and would also allow them to understand the situation they found themselves in. Having little access to the news or social media, desperate people were leaving their homeland to flee in search of safety to even more dangerous places, including active conflict zones in places like Yemen.

Many people had gone to Iraq, Somalia and Afghanistan before me, many people had run marathons before me, but nobody had run long distances unsupported through all three of the most dangerous war zones in the world. The idea ignited something passionate in me. It's not so easy these days to raise money for charitable giving with all the competition with this expedition or that record-break or world first. I needed something that would spark the imagination of potential donors, something that was more creative and innovative than usual, an idea that pushed a few boundaries. But most importantly, I needed an adventure that would inspire hope in the next generation of children in these countries. My plan was to attempt to complete a ten-kilometre run in Somalia, a half marathon in Iraq and a full marathon in Afghanistan, raising money beforehand and along the way for children's education in war zones. I really wanted to inspire some true hope in the next generation, and I knew I could if the plan materialised the way I wanted it to.

Of course, most people thought I was just crazy to even contemplate running through three of the most dangerous places on the planet. I will admit to thinking the same thing at times, but then I'd remember how beautiful some of these places are and how ignorant the general public can be about these countries. It's not all war, doom and gloom; the scenery and the people are actually quite lovely. The Western political narrative denies the beauty that can be found within the people and the places themselves.

For myself, I wanted to be able to feel something again, something deep and visceral, something to wipe out the depression and the anxiety that I'd been weighed down by for so long. Being a former soldier and having been in several dangerous situations fighting pirates off the coast of Somalia, I was vitally aware of the intense feelings you can experience when you're thrust out of your comfort zone. For me, that's when the magic starts to happen and the fun begins. I always feel more alive in an extreme environment, a conflict zone or when I'm surrounded by risk. My world becomes smaller, like looking through tunnel vision, and I zone into a hyper-vigilant state. My senses are heightened to a supernatural level where everything I feel, touch or hear is magnified and my body is flooded with adrenaline and cortisone. It's definitely addictive.

Although I love meeting new people and mixing with the crowd, I've always appreciated a certain level of solitude. It's good for my mental health. I'm quite happy with my own company and my own sense of peace. Walking or running alone is good for my soul and an extremely nourishing activity. I use that space for contemplating life, for planning, for problem solving and for generally blowing the cobwebs away. Never underestimate the power of fresh air and the rush of endorphins you get from running across fields and up hills. Running has enormous benefits psychologically, emotionally and physically and the act of getting into a routine and developing a positive habit helps me when the old anxious mind comes knocking.

Having made the conscious decision to run through Somalia, Iraq and Afghanistan, it was now time for the hard part – the actual planning of the expedition. Logistics is often the hardest part of any major expedition, especially when you need sponsors and funding. My major issue was convincing people to believe in me, get on board and to see the value in the expedition. The first hurdle was to believe in myself, that I could actually do this thing. If I couldn't do that I was fucked from the outset.

At the time of writing, the five most dangerous territories in the world are listed as Somalia, Iraq, Afghanistan, Syria and Yemen. I chose to run in the first three because by coincidence they were the three countries I had previously visited, served and worked in, and which I knew relatively well. I wanted to show people that these countries were more than just bullets, bombs and bad guys – that these countries are populated by a lot of good people with incredible stories of humanity, who simply want to live normal, violence-free lives. The landscape was also beautiful and prime to be admired. It was far more than endless desert sands, rough terrain and stark mountain passes. The one thing that lodged firmly in my mind was the look on the faces of the children I'd seen and experienced in these post-conflict zones. It was these faces and their stories that I wanted to show the world. It was these faces for which I wanted to raise money for educational opportunities. I needed to do something for these children because ultimately they were – and still are – the innocent victims of war, and every time one of those faces swam before my eyes I saw the face of my own daughter.

I shared my plans and my journey with Evie. I made sure

not to highlight the dangers because I didn't want her to worry about me, but I did want her to understand how privileged and lucky she was to be born in the West, to have the peace and serenity of a safe bed at night and a free education in a school with walls and a roof. I always encourage her to look at the bigger picture, to widen her horizons and think beyond her own singular world. I admire her for tackling the fundraising challenge head on with her home-baked cake sale which raised £23 right outside her mum's front door. One day, she generously offered all her pocket money to a homeless man begging on the streets of Andover, saying, 'He needed it more than me, Daddy...'

The planning process of the expedition itself was quite arduous. At the heart of it all was a charity project which obviously needed viable funding and then public exposure and a rigorous public relations plan. It was a case of 'Who do I know in these countries and who there can help me get this project off the ground?' One of the major issues was securing sponsorship and getting the appropriate insurance. Funnily enough, there aren't too many companies willing to insure people who voluntarily decide to visit and run in hostile environments. I spent a great deal of my time as a walking billboard with various company logos on my shirt, trying to secure media interviews and the like. Lloyd's of London offered help within its Hostile Environment Liability Protection scheme, fittingly abbreviated to HELP, and eventually donated $10,000 for the

Somali leg of the expedition. Many other smaller sponsors followed, chipping in five hundred quid here, a thousand quid there. All the money raised supported charities such as War Child, the Darlington Gacmadheere Foundation, UNICEF, Epilepsy Action and Frontline Children. Other sponsors donated material goods such as running shoes, running kit, satellite phones and tracking equipment, plane tickets, nutritional products and so on.

Our brilliant sponsors covered everything that was necessary to get this expedition off the ground from flights to accommodation and even insurance. I was keen to get directly in front of people and explain the ethos behind the expedition rather than just send email pitches and requests for sponsorship. I found people far more open to new ideas once they experienced my passion for the project and understood what I wanted to achieve. Personal contact is much more powerful and engaging and I was pleasantly surprised that so many people were willing to get behind me to become personally involved in the journey. Passion, after all, is infectious and addictive. My dealings with expedition supporters were and still are long-term and based on mutually beneficial relationships and regular communication. I make sure to keep them updated on the literal and metaphorical journey with me every step of the way.

I was anxious to get as many high-profile people on board

as I could; people like Dame Kelly Holmes were a bonus. Her support was particularly relevant, being formerly in the military and a runner to boot. Kelly also had her own mental health challenges. Whenever she leaves a comment on my social media, the world can see I have support from serious influencers, which helps me hugely with creating awareness. I'll always appreciate that when I did the Great North Run, Kelly made a point of going out of her way to see me and wish me luck. Dame Kelly Holmes is now the Honorary Colonel of the Royal Armoured Corps Training Regiment, the very corps I used to serve in. Presenters like Kay Burley from Sky News have also been invaluable and given me great media opportunities and exposure. They have all encouraged and supported me in my endeavours and I'm grateful to each and every one of them. I'm honoured and privileged to call people like them my good friends.

CHAPTER SEVEN

THE SHOCK OF SEIZURE

While engaged in the initial planning stages for the Running Dangerously project, I was still working as a security consultant in the shipping industry. Everything was coming together and I was full of anticipation for the first leg, which was based on running 10k in Somalia. I'd taken some time out to deliver a series of motivational talks in the south of France with a couple of colleagues that I worked with. I was still moping around after a few depressive episodes, but generally life was OK and I was keeping myself active.

So it was a massive shock when I woke up unexpectedly in a private hospital, not understanding where I was or what had happened to me, with my mate Tom's worried face looming over me.

'Where the bloody hell am I?' I asked.

'Private hospital, mate. They charge by the hour. This is gonna bust a bollock.'

'Jesus Christ, get me out of here. I'll be broke by tomorrow!' I said.

I was confused and completely out of it. When Tom gave me a mirror, my bruised face with its smattering of purple- and yellow-hued bruises and a chipped tooth stared back. I thought I must have fallen flat on my face, taken a beating, been mugged or something. The last thing I remember was walking along a concrete promenade down by the docks. Now I was spitting blood from a split lip and I'd somehow managed to chew the insides of my mouth raw. My tongue felt like a piece of flayed meat.

'What happened to me?'

'Seizure, Jord,' replied Tom. 'Maybe an epileptic fit of some kind, they reckon. I found you bang out on the deck. Someone called an air ambulance so I came with you, thought you might need some help.'

The last thing I remembered was walking down the side of the dockyard. Tom had gone off to grab a bite to eat at a local café. He told me that when he returned he saw a right commotion going on, dropped his paper bag with his sandwich and coffee and rushed towards the scene, trying to be a bit of a hero and seeing if he could do anything to help. Apparently a load of French guys were scattered around me frowning in that stereotypical Gallic way and looking puzzled, while I was flat out and flailing on the ground. One of the men was straddling me and trying to give me CPR, clumsily pushing up and down on my chest and breathing heavily into my mouth. Tom said he looked like he didn't know what he was doing, so he pushed him away saying, 'Thanks, mate, but he's with me.' He could see I was having a seizure and pushed everyone back to give me air and allow me to finish having my moment. In the meantime, someone from the restaurant opposite had called an air ambulance. Due to the remote location we were in and the narrow winding alleyway, it would have taken for ever for a regular ambulance to come and rescue me.

In the end, the whole episode cost me in the region of 3,500 euros. Stupidly, I didn't have insurance. I thought just popping over to France wouldn't be too much of a risk, after all I'd survived active service in Iraq and fought off Somali pirates on the Horn of Africa. Tom and I still joke today that he's a bit of a bad-luck charm. He served with me in Iraq and was also with me for the dengue fever scenario. Every time I get on a plane with him I know some bad shit's going to happen at some point in the trip!

I got out of that hospital and back to the UK as quickly as I could. As soon as I got home to Andover I had a load of blood tests, CT scans, MRIs… the lot. I had never had a seizure before, this one happened completely out of the blue. I was still in shock and feeling confused about the whole thing. I did a lot of research on epilepsy and its effects and was surprised to learn that it's one of the most common neurological disorders in the world, and that one in twenty-six people will develop epilepsy in their lifetime.

Tonic-clonic seizures are the most common type of epileptic seizure. They are also known as 'grand mal' seizures and include loss of consciousness, which lasts about ten to twenty seconds. This is usually followed by muscle convulsions and contractions which cause the person to fall down and usually continue for less than two minutes. Some people scream or cry out at the beginning of a seizure and lose bowel or bladder control, followed by a period of confusion and disorientation. Chronic headaches and intense sleepiness often follow. But what particularly interested me in my own diagnosis was the knowledge that seizures can be complicated by psychological problems such as depression and anxiety. Perhaps I wasn't doing as well mentally and emotionally as I thought. Many people will only have one such seizure in their lifetime. Others may need daily anti-seizure medications to prevent a recurrence. I sincerely hoped I was in the former category, because I was right pissed off that I had to give up driving for a time, and God only knew what this meant for the future of the expedition.

The NHS doctors, much as they tried, could find no obvious reason for my seizure. 'We've noticed nothing untoward in your scans, Mr Wylie. These things are often caused by abnormal electrical activity in the brain. Sometimes they are triggered by other health problems like extremely low blood sugar, a high fever or a stroke, but we honestly can't find any of these issues in your situation.' The reason behind my seizure was all a bit of a mystery.

It took a good six to eight weeks for me to fully recover. Then, just before Christmas that same year, I was staying with a friend up north when I suffered a second seizure. I'd been lying on his sofa, having a laugh and enjoying myself. My mate had popped out to the corner shop for a loaf of bread and a pint of milk, when I blanked out for probably about five minutes. When I came to, I had a cut-up mouth and a fat, swollen tongue where I had bitten down hard with my teeth. I was still lying on the sofa in the same prone position with a sliver of bloody dribble on my T-shirt, when my mate returned. He was none the wiser and never noticed a thing, but it worried me enough to know I had to report this second seizure. I couldn't just ignore it and pretend this wasn't going to affect the rest of my life.

I decided to pay a visit to a private doctor for a definitive answer. I had an expedition to plan and a challenge to complete, and to say I was concerned was a serious understatement. I saw an epilepsy specialist named Kim, who confirmed that the scans and blood tests showed no evidence of any brain abnormality, but she decided to take things one step further and have a good old dig around in my medical records. 'Something's not right, Jordan,' she said. 'You have no family history of epilepsy, but I see you had dengue fever two and a half years ago. That might be the problem right there.'

She presented me with evidence of a strong link between contracting dengue fever, then having seizures and eventually full-blown epilepsy. This was it then – the only logical explanation we could find for me having two seizures on the trot. dengue fever had taken more of a toll on me than I expected – and the timing couldn't have been worse.

I was concerned about how these seizures were going to affect my plans for the Running Dangerously expedition. To me, the physical aspects of the seizures were a mild irritant and inconvenience, but my financial supporters would be rightly concerned and my family would be worried. Just to be on the safe side, I decided to discuss any implications for the expedition with my NHS doctors. I explained the ethos behind the project, what it was, why I was doing it – how it was the opportunity to run long distances through three of the most dangerous places in the world to raise awareness and money for kids' education in war-torn territories. I was proud of the expedition and eager to talk about it to anyone who would listen and give me encouraging words. I didn't hold back and was bubbling over with excitement to get my news out there.

I almost laughed at the look on the doc's face. 'Whoa, hold on there, Mr Wylie. You surely can't be serious?' he asked. 'You absolutely cannot do this right now. In fact it would be downright dangerous, irresponsible and reckless for you to continue with this. The stress on your body, not to mention the heat exhaustion and the potential threat of dehydration, could trigger a significant and dangerous epileptic seizure. You intend to be out there in fierce terrain with absolutely no help or support. No, Mr Wylie, you're simply going to have to give up on this idea, however laudable it is. I'm very sorry.'

Shit. What was I going to do now? The expedition had progressed too far to give up at this stage. I had sponsors. I had people relying on me. I'd done a slew of media interviews on TV and radio. I'd spoken to journalists from national newspapers and magazines who had eagerly run my story of the intended project. I had about £25,000-worth of funding. Giving up on all that now was inconceivable. There had to be a way through this. I wasn't afraid, but neither was I going to be unrealistic and put myself and possibly others in danger. I determined to manage the risks and prepare in the best possible way and see what unfolded. I demanded it of myself. I simply couldn't give up at this point. If I did, I'd feel like a complete failure and slide back into an even deeper trough of depression. The planning, the organising, the sense of progression and the feeling of 'being the difference that makes a difference' had done so much good for my mental health, I couldn't run the risk of losing it all now.

I had countless debates with the medical professionals about managing my epilepsy and the planned runs; I was exhausted. I was bloody minded, I was belligerent and I was annoying – but I was also determined to see it through. My old commanding officer's voice rang in my ears: 'See the job through, Corporal Wylie. Don't leave it half-finished.'

But I had to be truthful and put it out there to my supporters and friends that I had epilepsy and the expedition was now laced through with an extra layer of jeopardy. It would have been disingenuous and dangerous to hide the fact. Supporters, sponsors and funders could make what they wanted of it. If they deserted the project, so be it. But the irony was that as soon as the message got out there that I had epilepsy and I was determined not to let it stop me running through Somalia, Iraq and Afghanistan, the more support I got. A lovely woman named Chantal Spittells, from the communications team of the charity Epilepsy Action, saw an interview I did on TV and got in touch with me, asking me if I would like to become an ambassador for the charity. 'You're doing some very inspiring challenges and we think what you're doing is incredible,' she said. 'Having epilepsy doesn't have to ruin your life. If it's managed sensibly, there's no reason why life should change. I think your expedition can help others with epilepsy to see that it doesn't mean they can no longer follow their dreams and live life to the full.'

They were singing the same song as me and I was proud and excited to be invited to become an ambassador for Epilepsy Action. It's a role I take seriously, helping to raise money and awareness for the charity. Now nothing was going to stop me getting on with my plans for Running Dangerously – not epilepsy, not dengue, not depression, not anxiety. Nothing.

CHAPTER EIGHT

KEEP MOVING FORWARDS

After being invited to become an ambassador for Epilepsy Action, I spent time researching and learning as much as I could about epilepsy and its effects on everyday life. Epilepsy Action are a great bunch, a community of people committed to a better life for everyone affected by the condition. They do an awesome job offering high-quality, accessible health-care services, so that people with epilepsy have the support they need to manage their symptoms. Wider awareness and understanding of epilepsy is important so that people living with the condition are treated with fairness and respect.

Personally, I tried to embrace the whole diagnosis of epilepsy and take it in my stride. I hoped to show that many people with epilepsy can still do pretty much anything they want if they have the right attitude. My parents were probably more concerned about me than I was, in all honesty. I try not to worry about things I can't control as this just causes unnecessary problems and stress I can't do anything about. A friend of mine named Laura Deas returned as an Olympic medallist from the Winter Olympic Games. She gave me some advice a while back when I was struggling with my relationship with Laura. She said, 'If you can, control the controllables in your life and try not to worry about everything else. You'll find you will live a much happier and more fulfilling life.' This little nugget of advice stuck with me. No point sweating stuff that's out of your hands, is there?

A positive mindset is important for everyone, not just for those with epilepsy. I find positive thinking beneficial for my mental health. It helps me eliminate the paranoia and negative thoughts that cause my numbing depression and stress. I know from my own research and from many of those I've met with epilepsy that they worry about the effects it can have on their personal and professional lives. When you start thinking with a positive mind your whole attitude changes. You'll see your day-to-day environment in a new light. A positive mind also allows you to handle everyday situations far better. This includes all the ups and downs in life, as well as those little 'extras' faced from having epilepsy. I want to show anyone out there that for many people with epilepsy the condition will only become an obstacle if you allow it.

Apparently, doctors reckon that about 1 to 3 per cent of the worldwide population has some form of epilepsy. I was surprised to learn that it's one of the most common neurological disorders out there, both in the United States and the UK, and it's more prevalent than autism spectrum disorder, cerebral palsy, multiple sclerosis and Parkinson's disease combined. While most patients can successfully manage their epilepsy with medication, others can face uncontrollable seizures which need to be actively and positively managed. However, both doctors and patients agree: epilepsy is a treatable disease and it shouldn't deter most people from living a normal life. One of the aims of the Running Dangerously expedition became flying the flag for those around the world with epilepsy.

Around this time I learned a lot about epilepsy and its various manifestations. Some people smell strange scents or see colours or visual images. Some engage in strange behaviours like chewing, lip smacking and fidgeting. Other times, patients will simply become unresponsive and stare blindly into space. There's no one-size-fits-all seizure; in fact, some patients with epilepsy experience more than one type of seizure. Many people envision full-body convulsions when picturing an epileptic seizure, which can appear quite dramatic and frightening. Generalised epilepsy can manifest as jerking on both sides of the body, or as a staring spell with decreased responsiveness. Meanwhile, with focal epilepsy, symptoms vary, ranging from visual illusions or hallucinations such as seeing auras, multi-coloured patterns and blinking rapidly, to hearing voices and feelings of déjà vu. There's also a phenomenon called sudden unexpected death in epilepsy, in which a person with epilepsy dies without warning, while asleep. Although the underlying science is still being researched, doctors believe that this might be caused by an irregularity in heart rhythm, impaired breathing or fluid in the lungs. People with epilepsy might consider sleeping on their backs and using wristwatches or bed alarms to detect seizures during sleep. When I learned all of this, I realised I had got off pretty lightly with my two seizures; some people have a much rougher ride than me, that's for sure.

I was surprised to learn how many well-known people live successfully with epilepsy. They range from entertainers and sports stars to politicians such as the late singer Prince and Theodore Roosevelt, the twenty-sixth President of the United States.

Florence Griffith Joyner, better known as Flo-Jo, the flamboyant American sprinter who won three gold medals at the 1988 Seoul Olympics after a meteoric rise to fame, died aged only thirty-eight during an epileptic seizure. Sadly, people don't often remember her fantastic achievements, but they do remember her form-fitting bodysuits and six-inch fingernails.

Athletes with epilepsy are particularly great at inspiring others to succeed in the face of a physical disability. Among some of the most inspiring is Chanda Gunn, the goalie for the 2006 women's US Olympic ice hockey team. Diagnosed at the age of nine, Chanda was already an avid athlete. When she was forced to give up swimming and surfing, she took up hockey and never looked back. For Gunn, in the same manner as myself, it's important to let other people with epilepsy know that the condition won't hold you back from your dreams. While ice hockey might be considered dangerous for people with epilepsy, Gunn demonstrates that anything is possible. 'There's no reason why a person with epilepsy can't play sports or pursue their dreams. I've learned to live with it, the fear of the unknown, because I want to really live life and for me that means playing ice hockey.' Today, Gunn is one of the most successful women in US hockey. She's also a spokeswoman for the Epilepsy Therapy Project. I feel honoured to have met her and I for one am inspired by her positive approach to all aspects of her life.

What struck me the most about my research into people with epilepsy is the amount of high-flyers who have the diagnosis. There seems to be a common thread: many people with the condition are high achievers who want to continue their normal lives and they don't allow epilepsy to stop them. It's a pretty special club and I'm certainly proud to be a member of it!

I'm also the brand ambassador for an organisation called ROAD iD who make wristbands for runners, outdoor enthusiasts and athletes. Since being diagnosed with epilepsy in January 2018, I now wear a wristband with my name, medical condition, emergency contact details, date of birth, blood group and date of last seizure. I encourage anyone with a medical condition to wear one of ROAD iD's wristbands. They can literally save lives. They are essential for anyone with epilepsy, and in the case of having a seizure when you're on your own, it is much easier for those who find you and indeed the doctors who eventually treat you to understand immediately what the problem is.

In order to progress onwards with my plans for Running Dangerously, I had to design a foolproof safety system, a risk management plan, if you like. Epilepsy Action gave me a bunch of booklets outlining first aid for epileptic seizures that I could give to people I was working and running with on the expedition – just in case I suffered a seizure in the middle of a run out in the back end of nowhere. It takes the form of a smart little acronym: ACTION. When you're not so academically gifted, an acronym can be a great way of remembering things, especially when you work in the military. Anyway, it goes like this:

A   Assess the situation: are they in danger of injuring themselves? If so, then remove any nearby objects that could cause injury.

C   Cushion their head (with a jumper, for example, to protect them from head injury).

T   Check the time – if the jerking lasts longer than five minutes, you should call an ambulance.

I   Look for a medical bracelet or ID card. It may give you information about the person's seizures and what to do.

O   Once the jerking has stopped, put them on their side. Stay with them and reassure them as they come round.

N   Never restrain the person, put something in their mouth or give them something to eat or drink.

And, crucially, if you know it's a person's first seizure, if the seizure lasts for more than five minutes, or if one seizure appears to follow another without the person gaining consciousness in between, or the person is injured, or if you believe the person needs urgent medical attention, then call an ambulance.

I refused to let my epilepsy change the way I planned the expedition. I'd always been in the business of planning risk, especially in my role as a maritime security consultant. It was simply bread and butter work to me. I spent a great deal of time investigating the routes we would take and the support that was available, especially the medical requirements and the locations of the nearest hospitals and clinics.

It was about the choices and decisions I made and about minimising the impacts of those choices should they go wrong and I found myself in a bad situation. I learned how to train others in epilepsy management and I learned how to recognise any potential signs of an oncoming seizure, like feeling when my body is under stress or fatigued. I learned to recognise my own physical limitations and when to just stop. Pushing boundaries is all well and good, but when you're in a war or conflict zone you have to be responsible for yourself and others – especially when you are in a remote area and there's no chance of a helicopter swooping in to rescue you or an ambulance to come trundling down the road.

Going into countries like Somalia, Iraq and Afghanistan, I had to be as comprehensive yet compact as possible with the kit I was intending to carry. There's always an element of risk – it was called Running Dangerously for very good reasons! Epilepsy wasn't the only danger I would be facing and needing to prepare for. There were a hundred and one other risks that had to be taken into account. The fact I was a former soldier who had served in Iraq was probably the biggest risk of all. I was now a civilian going back into the danger zone and a prime, high-profile target for kidnap and ransom by al-Qaeda, al-Shabaab or the Taliban.

I was trying to get a lot of sponsorship and support, so the media were another potential problem. It was a bit of a chicken and egg situation. I needed the media coverage in order to attract the sponsors, but at the same time I had to keep quiet about locations and timings because I didn't want to alert any rogue fighters or insurgents to my plans. The media didn't care too much about this, however; they were after the story, fresh and hot off the press. They published what they wanted, when they wanted, and bugger the consequences.

Having sorted out the preparation side of the epilepsy and risk management for the expedition, it was now time to sort out the physical side of my body, in terms of strength and endurance. If I was going to survive running three successive long-distance runs in arid, dry conditions and not collapse in a heap of exhaustion, sweat and tears, then my fitness levels needed to be upped. I was going to have to put my thinking cap on and delve into my bank of contacts to find the right person to act as a sympathetic physical trainer.

CHAPTER NINE

EXERCISE IS THE BEST MEDICINE

Mind willing, body not so much. I had some intense work ahead of me to get match fit for some major running. To add to the madness and the danger, although I enjoyed running, I'd never actually run a full marathon before! This was a first for me in more ways than one. But I found that pushing myself and my body to its limits spurred me on. It kept the black dog of depression at bay and my blood pumping daily.

The exercise fed my brain oxygen, cleared my head, gave me space and time to think, and a healthy dose of fresh air. My issues were still there, but when I was running I would think about those same things, and somehow I was able to process them differently. I would start my run with all these negative, unhelpful thoughts, and after a mile or two they seemed to vanish into thin air. I allowed myself a thirty-minute run at the end of each day. All the shit that had gone on in my day fell away, whether it was Laura giving me abuse about not paying child maintenance on time (and rightly so, I must add), or forgetting to put a bottle of water in Evie's packed lunch, or forgetting to drop off that week's ballet money or the general stress of work. Running and exercise gave me the energy to make decisions about getting my life back together. I've always run on my own; I rarely run with others unless I have to. I prefer the peace of the open road with no interruptions, allowing me to think.

Many people all over the world experience some form of mental illness in their lifetime and some suffer with a vague sense of fear and nervousness all of the time. My anxiety led me into a pit of physical malaise which I needed the exercise and running to conquer. I didn't want the deep sadness and fear I was feeling to control my life. I desperately wanted to take back ownership of myself, my life and my decisions. The physical symptoms of my anxiety and depression alone were numbing enough – the chest pains, the dizzy spells, the throbbing headaches.

Running soon became a therapeutic activity. I ran to find a way to escape myself and my disabling thoughts, to ease the pain and lessen the hurt of losing my family. When I felt my life spinning out of control, running gave me a choice over how I moved and used my body and its motions. Just thinking of nothing but putting one step in front of the other and keeping my arms pumping gave me clarity of thought. As I ran, I felt more resilient and more able to cope with the anger and disappointment I was experiencing.

Studies have shown that aerobic exercise can be as effective as anti-depressants in treating mild to moderate depression. Plus there are added side effects like improved health and weight management. Exercise is a first-line treatment for depression. There's more to it than plain old endorphins, the opioid the body produces during certain activities like exercise. The emerging view of running to improve mental health also takes into account long-term structural changes in the brain as well as subjective states like mood and cognition. Science continues working to explain the theory behind what we runners already know from practice.

Reframing ruminations or thinking differently about hashed-over topics is one of the main appeals of running. When I'm running, the thoughts come in and out, and I worry less. I'm able to think about things objectively. I realise that the things I think are a huge deal aren't really so scary in the grand scheme of things. When I'm feeling overwhelmed, shifting from worst-case-scenario thinking to small, in-the-moment tasks and doing things that have a goal, like running a four-mile drag with three hills and a valley, kicks off a positive feedback loop that continues throughout the run and shifts my thinking and emotions out of the trench of negativity.

I started strength and endurance training with my old army mate, Rick Webb. When I left the army and began my career in maritime security, Rick stayed in and did a tour of Afghanistan. It was while on active duty there in 2012 that he lost his leg after stepping on an improvised explosive device. Although Rick was still in rehab, he was in the process of transitioning out of the army and looking to the future. He's a passionate fitness instructor and personal trainer, spends much of his time in the gym, competes in weightlifting competitions and enjoys giving talks to local schools. He was the ideal training partner for the project.

I found the structure and discipline involved in training for longer runs and marathons provided the order I was looking for. Endurance helped me turn my elusive sorrows into something more tangible – something I could understand and appreciate, like physical pain. I found the physical discomfort had a way of flooding my consciousness and stopping me thinking overly complex thoughts about doom-laden scenarios. It was the vital break from the pain of my daily life I needed and gave me the welcoming boost of energy necessary to just get through each black day.

We spent long, arduous hours together in the gym going through my fitness routine. He wrote out a clutch of personal training programmes for me to complete and advised me on nutrition for bulk, energy and stamina.

'I'm going to push you to your limits, Jord,' he said. 'Well beyond your comfort zone. You're going to end up begging me to give you a break. But I'm not going to quit and neither are you. Your mental drive and alertness alone are going to see you through the hell I'm going to unleash on your body.'

Suddenly, I was running more miles than ever, while also building my workouts and strength training. This was new territory for me, one that I fully embraced. The pay-off was tremendous; I was feeling fitter and leaner than ever. Each day I tried to run a little farther. I had read that increasing your mileage comes with several benefits, including increased capillary density, larger numbers of mitochondria, better use of fat as fuel, adaptations to muscle fibre and higher glycogen storage. The cellular-level changes that take place within your body as you run enable you to maintain your required pace for longer by using oxygen and energy production to make your body more efficient. I also learned that increasing your mileage takes a lot of effort and time. So, in order to increase my running volume by 25 per cent, I went from running eight hours a week to running ten hours a week. I had to fit my training in between work and family commitments, so usually found myself running first thing in the morning or later in the evening. By the time I crashed into bed at night, I was physically and mentally exhausted.

Adding volume to your mileage will, of course, increase the risk of injuries such as tendonitis, so I was mindful of running on softer surfaces like grass rather than tarmac for most of my mileage, although I would be running on harder road surfaces in Iraq. Fitting in time for suitable post-run exercises was also important. I made sure to fit in flexibility exercises and the odd massage when I could. Increasing my mileage safely was the best way to improve my aerobic activity so that I would be able to increase my speed endurance and sustain my pace in the upcoming runs for Running Dangerously.

I'm quite a big bloke, so I also needed to consider my diet because I was partial to a beer and the odd take-away curry or pizza. All this training required more food than I was generally used to eating, so the local supermarket became my new best friend. I tried to cut out the sugar and the beer and looked at bulking up with a richer protein diet including loads of chicken, fish, eggs and fresh veg. My shopping trolley soon became the envy of every health freak out there. Food is more than fuel for energy; it provides all the nutrients needed for cardiovascular health and speed recovery, so I began to think of food as medicine.

I also made sure to try and get a regular eight hours of sleep in, although this was not always possible with my busy schedule. I had been told that sleep deprivation makes you inattentive and also makes you feel like you've run farther and for longer than you actually have. (Take it from me, there is *nothing* worse than thinking you've run farther than you actually have.) Lack of sleep also affects your ability to manage and regulate your core body temperature and makes it harder to perform well in adverse weather and environmental conditions, which is something I was mindful of, knowing I'd soon be challenging myself running in super-hot and arid surroundings.

I wouldn't say I'm super-fit and I'm certainly no professional athlete who lives and breathes to train. I was, and still am, just an ordinary guy who tries to push and test his body and his mind beyond what most consider normal endurance. I try and achieve what people believe to be impossible. There are some people who live and breathe fitness. They watch every calorie and what's in this and what's in that, but I'm not one of those people. I enjoy my life. I love having a beer with my friends and a good old ruby down my local Indian on a weekend. But I also work hard. I train when I need to train and then I up my game for the challenge, whether it's running, rowing, cycling or swimming. I relish the challenge, but I need a target to aim for. That's why it's so important for me to have lines in the sand that I'm working towards. I'm not someone who particularly wants to go to the gym every day – I prefer competitive sports that have a clear winner or winning team. I would much rather take part in a footy match or play a game of cricket or basketball. I like to win, I'm very competitive. Everything I want to do, whether it's a football match or a pub quiz, I have to win!

I worked out with Rick, using a lot of weights. Developing my core strength was vital, so I worked on my muscle development, abdomen, trunk, and lower back. Rick told me that lifting heavy weights, especially with the lower body, could improve race times for longer-distance runners. He certainly put me through my paces, encouraging me to work on my abs, obliques, lower back, hips, quads, hamstrings, calves, Achilles tendons, shoulders and chest muscles – the lot. I used kettle-bells and my own weight as a counter-balance. Other training toys included balance boards and industrial-strength elastic bands. I did quite a lot of hill running with the aim of developing stronger hip flexors, and I found that hill reps of about ten seconds on a steep gradient were just as effective as squats and lunges to build lower-body strength and power.

Rick knew all about the planned expedition and what we were hoping to achieve with our fundraising efforts, and he wanted to be in at ground level. He had been in the same regiment as me, the King's Royal Hussars, and he too had seen first-hand how a child is affected in a war zone and the chaos it can cause. He told me there were some six million children around the world who have been displaced or affected by war. The prime focus of the adults is obviously on the children's survival, with their access to education coming second to their brutal day-to-day existence. This statistic alone spurred both Rick and me on. It brought home the fact that money – even relatively small amounts of money – can achieve great things on the front line and go some way to making significant changes in these children's lives.

One of my biggest concerns was not just the security considerations, but the brutality of running in the sweltering climate of the Middle East and East Africa; I'd never run in extreme climates before. A lot of my heat production would be coming from my thighs, so I knew I'd have to make it a priority to stop the heat building up. It wasn't so much the pace I was concerned with, but the amount of time I would be running in such harsh terrain. Your primary source of energy during a marathon is glycogen, but your body can only store so much of the stuff. Rick warned me that as my glycogen levels fell, my muscles would begin to feel tired and heavy. As well as telling me about the need for constant hydration, he also suggested consuming small amounts of carbs in the form of gel chews to help me from hitting the dreaded wall, or 'bonking' as it's known in runner's world. It certainly had a different meaning back in Blackpool where I grew up!

Rick was as good as his word and pushed me hard to get the best out of me. After a week of training with him I was forced to admit that he might only have one leg, but at least he could still bloody well walk, which was more than I could. It occurred to me that this challenge might be a lot harder than

I thought. I wasn't sure I was going to be able to make it. There was a lot hanging on this expedition; a lot of people were cheering me on and I couldn't bear the thought of fucking it up. There was too much at stake, not least my mental health.

Rick had been diagnosed with PTSD after his last stint in Afghanistan and I think the training for the expedition gave him a new focus. Having both been in the military, and understanding each other's characters and what made us both tick, we bounced off each other mentally and emotionally. He advised me on what to expect from Afghanistan, especially the Taliban-infested mountains and the inherent danger I could be facing out there.

Rick was an integral part of the expedition and we shared a lot of common ground and understanding. We ultimately forged a solid friendship during those long weeks of pitiless training. Rick wanted to join me in Afghanistan. He needed to get back there in order to face his own demons, but his injuries prevented him from running long distances. Instead we contrived a master plan – Rick would run the final mile of the Afghanistan leg with me. A brave choice, but sadly when push came to shove, he wasn't physically able to join me, his injuries simply would not let him. He had a long way to go on the road to recovery and we certainly didn't want to compromise the great work he had done in his rehabilitation so far.

Rick wasn't the only athlete I called on to help me train and give me advice. Chris Thompson, the European silver medallist, was a long-distance runner who had run in a lot of hot countries in places like Qatar and Dubai. I reached out after following him on social media. I follow a lot of people who inspire me or motivate me in different ways. I like to observe how they conduct themselves and try to work out what their drivers are, with the aim of applying them to my own projects. Chris Thompson was somebody who really stood out to me. So, I introduced myself to him and told him about the Running Dangerously expedition and what we were trying to achieve with the project. Unfortunately, I also had to tell him that I wasn't in a financial position to be able to pay him for any time and help he might be willing to offer. But he's a top bloke and within a couple of hours of me contacting him he replied saying, 'Hey, Jordan, I've just reviewed your promotional video and what you're doing trying to help children is amazing. You're taking on a major feat here. I certainly don't envy you running where you're going, but I'd be delighted to support you in any way I can.'

I replied, telling him it would be great to be able to do some training sessions with him and get some tips for coping with running in hot climates. A week later we were on a running track together and I was running alongside the European silver medallist! He was a totally inspiring guy who gave me some great tips, all of which I took on board. To have someone of Chris's calibre supporting me gave me that extra kick. I had some real support now, it wasn't just my mates down the pub who don't really know that much about running, I had a member of the Team GB squad who's at the peak of his game and winning races all around the world rooting for me. Chris was usually training with Sir Mo Farah, but now he was training with Jordan Wylie. This was pretty special to say the least and I was delighted to be able to share in this man's wealth of experience. Soon after, I was speaking to Dame Kelly Holmes, who was a friend of Chris's, and to Jo Pavey, another British Olympian. These were the very people who had always inspired me and who were now tweeting messages of support.

When you're just an ordinary guy from Blackpool and you get a double Olympic champion sending you a message wishing you good luck, it gives you the kick to run 10k around the park when you'd far rather be back at home having a lie-in with a nice, hot cup of tea.

Getting fit for an expedition, as tough as it may be, is only one piece of the puzzle when it comes to planning. There are so many more aspects required to make any expedition or project a success, and perhaps even more so when there is a charitable motive behind it. The most important part of the Running Dangerously expedition was to get as many people, businesses and supporters on board to kindly sponsor me. I've found myself very fortunate in that regard as I have met some great people who really want to help make a difference in this world. If you're lucky enough to meet these types of people, hang on to them tightly and never let them go. They are dream-builders. Seriously, I mean it!

I always tell young adventurers who are looking to travel the world, or trying to pursue a world first, or perhaps break a record, that the actual expedition itself is the fun and sexy bit that everyone loves, but getting to the start line is where the real hard work is. With my planning endeavours, there were many challenges and issues to deal with. Unfortunately it's not always as simple as just jumping on a plane with a set of running shoes and away you go. If only!

Visas, letters of invitation, in-country travel, insurance, accommodation, cultural considerations, medical requirements, local agents, vehicle hire – the list goes on and on. The first time you normally find out you have forgotten or missed something is the moment you actually need it. This is why the military drill into you the famous seven P's from day one: Prior Preparation and Planning Prevents Piss Poor Performance.

Alongside all of the expedition ingredients for success I was also conscious that I had made a commitment to sponsors to provide some first-class exposure, which I am delighted to say I delivered with a TV documentary which aired on Forces TV, broadcast by Sky and Virgin in February 2019. I was forever speaking at events and giving motivational talks to my sponsors, clients and staff. To this day, I really enjoy this side of any project as I love meeting new people and helping to inspire them when and where I can through my own life lessons and adventures.

Eventually, all the planning finally came to a head. We were up and ready for the off… I didn't want to be known for just blasting hot air, so it was time to stop talking and start doing. Any drill sergeant in any army anywhere is known for yelling, 'Eyes front,' so now I had to shift to the active state of actually running in Somalia. Self-belief is a nice phrase, but if it's not backed up by action, it's pretty useless. The boxer Muhammad Ali once said, 'He who is not courageous enough to take risks will accomplish nothing in life.' I was ready to embrace the fear and leave any regrets outside the back door.

CHAPTER TEN

THE WORLD'S MOST DANGEROUS PLACE

I knew this leg was going to be bloody dangerous, but sitting in the old, clapped-out Toyota on the way to my hotel in Mogadishu, the capital of Somalia, I was somewhat guarded. My old friend anxiety was creeping up on me. I could feel his tendrils stroking the back of my neck. I was exhausted after a long trip flying from the UK to Paris, Paris to Ethiopia, Ethiopia to Djibouti and finally Djibouti to Mogadishu. I hadn't had enough to eat or drink and was dehydrated. The air, both inside and outside the car, was hot and dry, making it difficult to breathe. The view from the back of the car was dismal, the roadside littered with burnt-out vehicles, their mangled metalwork twisted into giant hooks. The road was still blackened with melted tar and sand, the low concrete buildings scarred with scorch marks.

The atmosphere was infused with despair. It was palpable and quite depressing. The media portrays Somalia as the world's most dangerous place, with prolonged suffering and chaos simmering beneath. Conflict, piracy, famine and terrorism are the words most associated with the country. Armed men were everywhere, looking menacing as they strutted in full view with their weapons slung across their chests and their tattered camo covered in sand and dust. The corruption was unhidden, staring me full in the face. I noticed several people handing over wads of cash to armed guards in order to get through the checkpoint without any hassle. The guards took the bribes without a backward glance, stuffing the notes into their jacket pockets. The windows in our car were blacked out for security. Our money was paid over and we got through without any guards checking the back of the car or inspecting the inside of the boot. It's common in parts of Africa to just get on with it, pay the money and ask no questions, so I wasn't unduly concerned. Nobody wants to cause any unnecessary problems.

Two months previous to my trip, on 14 October 2017, a large truck filled with explosives was detonated at a busy crossroads downtown in the Hodan District of Mogadishu, killing almost 600 people and injuring over 1,000 more. This was a massacre, a crime against humanity and the good people of this nation. The truck was detonated after it was stopped.

The actual target of the attack was understood to have been a secure compound housing international agencies and troops. Although no organisation claimed direct responsibility, officials stated that al-Shabaab, a jihadist fundamentalist group, was most likely responsible. This was not their first attack in Somalia and certainly wouldn't be their last.

The explosion took place on one of the busiest streets in Mogadishu, a road lined with government offices, restaurants and kiosks. Victims included senior civil servants, five paramedic volunteers, a journalist, an American-Somali man, a medical student and, sadly, fifteen children. The full death toll may never be known with certainty, as the remains of many people couldn't be found due to the intense heat – which, I was told, could still be felt almost a mile away from the scene for some time afterwards. Others were buried quickly by relatives, following strict Islamic custom.

Reliable sources close to the government claimed the truck was carrying 350kg of home-made and military-grade explosives. The truck had briefly been detained at a checkpoint, but was given the green light after local authorities vouched for it. It was then stopped by security officials while stuck in a traffic jam. Just as it was about to be searched, the driver put his foot down hard and accelerated, crashing through a barrier. The truck exploded in a massive ball of fire. At least two hotels collapsed in the vicinity, trapping scores of people under rubble, and the Qatari embassy was severely damaged.

The attack was the deadliest in Somalia's history, surpassing the Mogadishu bombing seven years before, which killed 100 people, and was one of the biggest attacks in the whole of Africa. Shocked, the Somali President, Mohamed Abdullahi Mohamed, declared three days of mourning in response to the bombings and joined thousands of people who responded to a desperate plea by hospitals to donate blood for the wounded victims.

But death and destruction wasn't the only problem here. Somalia was continuing to suffer its worst drought in forty years, with climatic calamity compounded by war and poor governance. Al-Shabaab, the prominent Somali insurgency group with alleged ties to al-Qaeda, banned humanitarian assistance in areas it controlled, forcing hundreds of thousands of people to choose between starvation or brutal punishment. The bombings occurred amid deep public discontent and political divisions between federal and regional leaders, forcing the US to designate Somalia a 'zone of active hostilities' and massively increasing their ground forces in Somalia.

So, here I was, newly arrived in Mogadishu, the most dangerous city in the world by many accounts, and about to go running in the lion's den. Scenes from the movie *Black Hawk Down* were swimming in my head and I was well aware of the risk, particularly the danger of kidnap for ransom, but I'd done my due diligence and my risk assessments and although I was nervous and anxious, I was still feeling relatively confident about the whole project.

I first visited Somalia back in 2009, when I was working in security, and I'd been intrigued by the country ever since. I had found it a fascinating land rich in heritage, culture and history. Situated on the east coast of Africa with its coastline stretching over 3,000 kilometres from the southern Indian Ocean right up through the notorious Gulf of Aden and on towards the Red Sea, I was now curious to see how the political and security situation had changed since my last visit. Somalia has been engulfed by violence and lawlessness since dictator Mohamed Siad Barre was toppled; it is believed that more than half a million people have been killed since the start of the civil war in 1991. The current phase of the Somali civil war was concentrated in southern Somalia, with the conflict between the forces of the Federal Government of Somalia assisted by African Union peacekeeping troops and various militant terrorist groups and factions. The violence displaced thousands of people in the southern part of the country and the conflict saw fierce fighting between the Sufi Ahlu Sunna Waljama'a and al-Shabaab.

Al-Shabaab means 'the youth' in Arabic. The faction emerged as the radical youth wing of Somalia's now defunct Union of Islamic Courts, which controlled Mogadishu before being forced out by Ethiopian forces. Unfortunately, the terrorist organisation has long tentacles and there are many reports of foreign jihadists going to Somalia to help al-Shabaab, from neighbouring countries as well as from the US and Europe. Al-Shabaab has imposed a strict version of Sharia law in areas under its control, including stoning to death women accused of adultery and amputating the hands of thieves. There have been numerous reports that al-Shabaab may have formed links with other militant groups in Africa, such as Boko Haram in Nigeria and al-Qaeda in the Islamic Maghreb, based in the Sahara Desert. Apparently, al-Shabaab debated whether to switch allegiance to the Islamic State (IS) group after it emerged, but it rejected the idea and a small group of fighters broke away from the main group. Al-Shabaab is currently led by Ahmad Umar, also known as Abu Ubaidah, and the US has issued a gigantic $6 million (£4.5 million) reward for any information leading to his eventual capture.

A crippling drought caused by lack of rainfall back in 2010 threatened the lives of millions of people living in low-lying areas of Somalia, particularly in the provinces of Lower Shabelle and Bakool, which the United Nations later declared a famine zone. Sadly, these provinces have experienced a blinding increase in prices for staple items such as bread, milk, sugar and paper. Tens of thousands of people have died and almost one million people have fled across the border into overcrowded and disease-ridden refugee camps in Ethiopia,

Kenya and Djibouti. Tragically, I have seen first-hand that many of these people include very young children who have been displaced by conflict.

Needless to say, security for foreigners is hard to guarantee in Somalia. The US Department of State warns all US citizens against all travel to Somalia, as does the British Foreign Office travel advisory service, whose website advised at the time of writing: 'In the southern and central regions, there is ongoing serious violence, dangerous levels of criminal activity and general internal insecurity. We advise any British citizens in Somalia to leave immediately.' Naturally, I took their advice with a pinch of salt…

But, aware of the official requirement for all foreigners to be accompanied by an armed guard, I'd previously arranged for my agent and driver, Hussein, to keep me out of too much trouble. He was a contact from my old days working in the anti-piracy network and I trusted him. Local intelligence and local information was worth more to me than anything I was ever going to see or hear on the news. The power of local knowledge is invaluable, because the news usually manipulates information to suit Somali or, indeed, Western audiences, whereas the guys on the ground will tell me what had happened, when it happened, where I needed to be and what I needed to be looking out for. Keeping my network alive has always proved invaluable and it's something I continue to nurture on a regular basis.

It would have been a suicide mission if I didn't have security, but it was also a double-edged sword because although I obviously needed security, I also wanted to keep a low profile. The moment you've got security, you've immediately got an armed team of men with guns flagging up the fact you're somebody important – a Westerner, a journalist or maybe even a tourist, although the latter were few and far between in this part of the world. It was important to find the right balance between being secure, but at the same time not drawing lots of attention to myself. This wasn't easy. The last thing I wanted was to be snatched by a band of armed insurgents and stuck in a boilersuit in some godforsaken place with the prospect of my head being chopped from my shoulders. I preferred to keep a low profile and have a few trusted contacts as opposed to having a six-man armed security detail protecting my vehicle. It's normally the police, the military, the security services who are prime targets, anyway. The reality was that if I did find myself in the shit, I'd be isolated with no one hurrying to help bail me out.

Hussein dropped me off at the Sahafi Hotel in the afternoon. For years the hotel has served as the gateway to one of the world's most dangerous countries for foreign journalists and the rare, brave businessman. Even in the hardest times, the staff manage to provide clean rooms and good food and the restaurant is noted for a good lamb chop, too. Nestled in the dusty streets, the hotel is one of the more popular and safer hotels in Mogadishu, although most hotels have experienced some form of security incident over the years. It looked rather utilitarian with its four floors of chequerboard windows but I'd been told that if you can convince customs of your sanity, then it was the best hotel to stay at.

We drove through the main gate of the hotel and up to a gathering of armed security guards. They did a typical security search, flipping the boot and bonnet of the car and giving my passport a cursory glance. I had the feeling my passport could have said Mickey Mouse for all they cared. They checked my bags and Hussein bunged them $10, as if to say, 'We're all good here, fellas.'

You need to take personal security very seriously when you're in a country like Somalia because you can't rely on the national security or the hotel security. You've got to be thinking security, security, security, all the time from your own personal perspective. If you relied on the security services the hotel was providing, I think you'd be living a very dangerous lifestyle. Corruption is often quite high in these places. You never quite know if the person shaking your hand in the market in the daytime could also be the person who will try to kill you in the night. You have to treat everyone with a bit of caution, as a possible risk or a threat, and behave and act accordingly.

Hussein checked me in at the hotel reception and got my passport scanned. 'Get some rest,' he said. 'I'll pick you up in the morning and we can do a recce of the routes you're going to run. Make sure everything is going to be OK.' The fact this man was using words such as 'recce' reminded me from my interactions with him many years ago that he was still very tactically aware and was familiar with working with both military and law enforcement personnel. I had a free day the following day and wanted to do some sight-seeing and get a feel for the local culture.

I took the stairs up to my room. Apart from the really luxurious ones, most five-star hotels in Africa are the equivalent of two- or three-star hotels in Europe, but I was pleased to see my room was clean and I even had my own toilet. The double bed in the centre of the room, with its low-slung thin mattress and grey coverlet, was covered in a mosquito net. The place was literally buzzing, but the overhead fan was broken and the air con was down. Every so often the generator would crank to life and I'd get a bit of relief from the heat and a couple of hours' access to the internet. After two intense days of travelling, I was feeling worn out and bruised, so decided to have a shower and try to get a bit of kip for a couple of hours before dinner. I was woken by the muezzin's melodic call to evening prayers from the nearby mosque, a sound I've always found atmospheric and soothing. I got dressed in fresh clothes and made my way downstairs to the dining area for my evening meal.

I was sitting quietly on my own, reflecting on the adventure to come, drinking local coffee and waiting for my food to arrive – the obligatory meat and rice – when a smart, well-suited and booted gentleman approached me. I thought he must be someone important because I instantly noticed the bodyguard with an earpiece standing vigilantly behind him. 'I saw you sitting alone,' he said in excellent English, 'and I wondered what has brought you here to my hotel. I like to get to know my guests. Allow me to introduce myself. My name is Abdifatah Abdirashid and I am the owner of this hotel. You are most welcome.' The other diners and staff members were making way for him and looking at him in the most respectful manner; he was obviously the main man.

We shook hands and Abdi, as I called him, and I got chatting. I was well aware of the element of risk, because every person you chat to is likely someone who could tell your story to someone else who may have an ulterior motive. Anyway, there had been so much media coverage about the Brit coming to run in Somalia that it didn't take Abdi too long to work out who I was and what I was doing there. I told him the complete story of what I was up to in Somalia and my intention to run 10k in order to raise money for kids' education and international awareness of their survival among the ruins and turmoil of his war-torn country. He looked at me as though I was off my rocker! He nodded at me warily and said something about how noble my project was and how grateful he was that I intended to do something for the children in his country. Then he abruptly said, 'Goodnight', turned on his heel and left me sitting alone to finish my dinner, somewhat perplexed at his hasty departure.

The following morning, after a good night's sleep and before I went down to breakfast, I heard a sharp rap at my hotel room door. I opened the door to find a serious-looking Abdi standing there. I couldn't decide if he looked crestfallen or angry, his face was quite red. 'Mr Jordan,' he said, 'I cannot let you do this. It is far too dangerous. I could never forgive myself if I failed to warn you of the dangers of your endeavours. I am a digester of information, you see, Mr Jordan. I had to sleep on what you told me last night, to work it all out in my mind and I am telling you now – it is far, far too dangerous for you. Please, you must reconsider, Mr Jordan, I beg you.' The kind, gentle, calm Abdi of last night had gone, to be replaced by a stern general talking to his rookie lieutenant. This new Abdi was deadly serious.

'It's a bit too late for that Abdi, sir.' I replied. 'Everything's sorted. People are relying on me.'

'I'm not happy. I feel I have a responsibility to warn you that my own dear father, Abdirashid Mohamed, was killed here, blown to pieces by a car bomb two years ago. I know you have worked in security and safety, have done all your risk assessments and explored your route, but I tell you again, it's really not safe, this is Mogadishu now, my friend. It is a beyond crazy idea, Mr Jordan, and I fear you may be a prime terrorist target.'

'Honestly, don't worry about me, Abdi. I've spent half my life in these places. I know what I'm up against,' I replied.

'Well, I am sorry to inform you then, Mr Jordan, that if you insist on this most dangerous endeavour, then you will no longer be welcome in my hotel.'

Abdi's adamant warning rang in my ears and I felt the familiar skin prickle of anxiety. The place was, after all, littered with the remnants of car bombs, broken buildings and absolute chaos. Perhaps I ought to reconsider, perhaps I had been too hasty in my preparations. After all, more than 500 innocent people had been murdered in cold blood just a few months previously and the general feeling in the city was still extremely tense and hostile.

When Hussein came to pick me up for our recce, he wandered into the breakfast area and saw me speaking once again with Abdi. He came right over. He and Abdi walked away from me and started talking directly to each other in Arabic. I couldn't understand a word, but it was almost like they were having an almighty argument. Their heads were bobbing backwards and forwards and their hands were gesticulating wildly like frenzied marionettes. To me, a polite and generally respectful Brit, it looked like these two guys were having an extremely heated conversation.

'Er, is everything OK, guys?' I asked, with classic British understatement. But both Abdi and Hussein completely ignored me and continued their animated dialogue. It turned out that Hussein was not at all happy that Abdi had advised me against running in Mogadishu. I didn't know if that was because he wouldn't get paid his daily rate plus expenses if I buggered off, or if he was genuinely looking out for me. Something told me it was probably the former.

'This is no problem, Mr Wylie, no problem. We can simply find a safer location in Mogadishu for you to run, simple,' said Hussein.

'I don't know, I don't really want to just go out in the sticks somewhere and run on my own. Part of the reasoning behind all this is to embrace the local culture, meet the people, raise the profile of our expedition and what we're trying to do.'

'No, no, we can go into the desert and you can run there. It will be perfectly safe, trust me, I even have family living there, my friend.'

The idea of running 10k on my tod in the middle of nowhere didn't really appeal and I was beginning to feel despondent when Abdi piped up with an alternative plan. 'I have seen on the internet plans for the first ever mixed-gender 10k race in Hargeisa in Somaliland in a few weeks' time. Why don't you consider joining in and running there? It is far safer in Hargeisa, quite peaceful, really, and you will still be able to raise funds and awareness of our situation with no problems.'

I thanked Abdi for his suggestion and left him back at the hotel while I went out for coffee in the city with Hussein, a new plan brewing in my mind. I didn't discuss it with Hussein because I still needed him on my side to ferry me around and I didn't want to piss him off. We spent the rest of the day down by the port speaking to a few locals. There were what seemed like a million fishermen all lined up along the harbour area trying to sell the same catch of the day. I don't know how they do business because they're all trying to sell the same kind of fish and all the vendors are shouting out and battling against each other. We ended up buying a truly massive swordfish for an over-inflated Westerner's price. Hussein whacked it in the boot of the car and we took it back to the hotel where they were having a barbecue that night. The chef was very grateful and happily shared it with the remaining guests. It was sublime – perhaps the best fish I've ever tasted, which, on reflection, may be precisely why they can all sell the same fish in the same spot!

After the barbecue, I spent that evening alone in my hotel room, mulling over Abdi's advice and looking into the race in Hargeisa on the stuttering internet. It was a way out of the danger zone and – because I wasn't totally crazy – I was prepared to re-think my running plans. The company organising the run was a British outfit called 'Untamed Borders' and they specialised in travel to extreme locations. But Hargeisa was massively far north of Mogadishu. It would be a right pain in the arse to get there and I didn't have a clue where to start.

I banged out an email to the organiser, a guy called James Willcox, asking how I could become a competitor in the race. He emailed straight back. 'Feel free to get involved,' he wrote.

'We're trying to get international runners to join. There won't be many of you running, so your enquiry is perfect timing.'

It didn't take me long to reconsider, hence the swift change of plan. James said he would arrange all the logistics apart from the flights, that was down to me. When I told Abdi he was thrilled to bits, slapping me on the back with a grin from ear to ear. His dire warnings about the dangers of running in Mogadishu had been heard and now he could relax. He also kindly waived my total hotel bill. He was an absolute gentleman, that man.

I had a couple of free days before I needed to fly to Hargeisa so I asked Hussein to take me on a visit to an orphanage in Mogadishu. I wanted to see the conditions the kids were living in first-hand and where our funds were going, plus I wanted to get to know a few of the volunteers managing the place. With the country slowly recovering from years of armed conflict and repeated droughts and crop failures, life is extremely hard for Somali kids. In addition to the violence, the frequent periods of drought and food shortages have led to repeated famine, meaning Somalia now has one of the highest malnutrition rates in the world. Children often lack the necessary food for them to grow healthily and many families don't have access to simple medical treatment and advice. Many families are internally displaced and have lost their livelihoods and it's the children who are hit the hardest by the precarious situation in the country.

Clans and warlords have controlled Mogadishu and other parts of the country for many years, and fighting between Somalia's Transitional Federal Government forces, supported by African Union troops, and other insurgent groups such as al-Shabaab, have been going on for decades. Southern and central Somalia have been most severely affected by these armed conflicts. Al-Shabaab have been accused of recruiting child soldiers as young as ten and of abducting young girls to fight, become domestic slaves or be taken as wives for adult soldiers. Those children who have lost or been separated from their parents or carers are the most vulnerable to falling into the hands of insurgent groups.

Most of the orphans on the streets of Mogadishu I saw were aged from about four up to fifteen years. I'd seen many for myself daily, either milling around the market or offering to shine shoes for scraps of food. They would tug at my sleeve, 'Shiny shoe, mister, shiny shoe?' The Somali government pledged to ban the recruitment of child soldiers in areas it controls, but, without any plans to integrate these children into the community, all those former child soldiers have nowhere to go and are now living on the streets, using drugs, scavenging for food and recycling materials from the town dump to sell for a pittance. It's the 'lucky' ones who find themselves cared for in one of the under-funded and under-staffed orphanages. Since 2001, many Islamic charities that catered for the country's most vulnerable children have been shut down after their funding was cut. Sadly, since the tragedy of 9/11, several Islamic charities lost their funding from the Gulf States after the US wrongly branded Islamic charities as supporters of terror activities, wiping out funding for the many reliant orphanages in Mogadishu.

I found that few children in Mogadishu go to school on a daily basis as most schools have been destroyed or closed because of the incessant violence in the city. For the most part, lone children face the struggle of surviving on their own. It shocked me to learn from some of the elders I spoke to that more than 1,500 children had been orphaned as a result of the recent vicious bomb attack in Mogadishu. Hussein took me to one of the local orphanages in the city and, true to my expectations, it was pretty grim to say the least. The place looked like something out of a movie, more like Guantanamo Bay than a home for orphaned children. It was nothing more than a rudimentary prison, stinking of shit too. It was disgusting. The kids slept thirty to a room in old, crappy metal bunk beds. Each room had one smelly toilet and one wardrobe for all thirty kids to share. The flooring was a mixture of cracked old linoleum or compacted dried mud mixed with dung. There was no electric light, so the kids relied on the little natural daylight that seeped through the windows and the cracks in the walls.

The main living and eating area consisted of a small kitchen with a few tables where the kids sat and did occasional simple lessons. The whole place was staffed by volunteers. There was no money for upkeep and limited resources in terms of cooking equipment, clothes and the basic necessities of life. A few books were scattered among the dead cockroaches. I can't say it was well maintained, but the staff did their best and I was surprised to see so many smiling faces. The kids were more than happy to see a visiting stranger, a new face and a new pair of hands they could high-five. They seemed content, unaware of any other life and, to be honest, being in that place was probably far better and safer than being out there on the violent streets of Mogadishu. It put it all into perspective when I considered that just on the other side of the fence, over 500 people had recently been bombed to bits. Who was I to judge the state of the orphanage? Still, witnessing that kind of deprivation pissed me off no end and by the time Hussein and I got back in the car I was more determined than ever to try and help with funding and give these kids a smidgeon of hope and help towards a more comfortable life.

I ended up walking round the marketplace on my own, just to clear my head, but I got more than I bargained for. I was busy looking at the produce on one of the stalls, happily haggling on a pile of over-ripe fruit, when I heard gunshots that were far too close for comfort. I knew I had to get out of there and fast. Everyone suddenly scattered in a panic, stallholders ducked below their canopies, any children previously playing in the street were nowhere to be seen. They all knew their exit routes and nobody was hanging around to find out who was firing – or why. Fortunately, I was near a major road and flagged down a taxi immediately, yelling to the driver to get us out of there. But the driver didn't speak a word of English, and started to drive towards the sound of the shooting. I tried to tell him, 'No, no, you've got to go the other way,' but because he didn't understand what I was saying, he just shrugged his shoulders and carried on driving the same way. He seemed entirely unfazed by the sound of the shooting. It was an everyday occurrence to him and his unconcern surprised me. I ended up having to show him my business card with the name of my hotel on it so that I could get back to a safe area. I later found out that the commotion was just the security forces dealing with a local incident. Petty crime is rife in Mogadishu and tragically lives are taken every day as result. I can't imagine what it must feel like for civilians living under those sort of pressures day in and day out, but as far as I could see they just took it in their stride and learned to deal with it, incorporating it into their day-to-day living.

After that incident, Hussein stuck to me like glue, keeping a tight watch on me. I got chatting to one of the ladies running a clothing market stall who was telling me about the football shirt initiative, 'Kits for Kids', one of the major charities which donates second-hand football shirts for the football-mad kids and adult men in Somalia. There was me thinking what a great job the Brits were doing, donating their football shirts, when she gave me a disgruntled look. 'What you don't understand,' she said, 'is that it's all very well these big UK and European charities sending stuff over, thinking they are helping out, but what happens in reality is that nobody then wants to buy things off the market and we can't make a living. If we can't make a living, we can't feed our families, it is just not fair.'

That thought hadn't occurred to me before, but she was dead right. We just think, yep, we'll donate clothes or whatever, but don't recognise that it affects the local economy. As far as I know, no one's done an impact study on the local results of charitable giving on the second-hand clothes market. I had a lot to learn… and Hargeisa beckoned.

• • •

There was a sad postscript to my visit to Mogadishu. Just over twelve months later I was in the living room of my friend's house in Blackpool. It was Remembrance Sunday, November 2018. To me, as a former soldier, Remembrance Day is one of the most important days of the year. It's the day where you get to re-engage with people who you've spent a lot of time with in your life and your career. It's that *Band of Brothers* sort of thing. It's obviously a time for remembrance and reflection, but it's also a time where if you've served in the military, you get to very proudly wear your uniform, your medals and your regimental tie once again. You spit and polish your shoes, have a shave, comb your hair and feel great pride in being part of the military family again for that one day a year. Remembrance Day is always one of the first dates I mark on my calendar every year, without fail.

Normally I would go up to Blackpool and march with my dad. We've had a reunion every Remembrance Day for the past ten years. All the guys in my old regiment who lived in the northwest and beyond would come together in that seaside town which will always be my home – good old Blackpool. It's a great day out for a few beers as well as a day of remembering our fallen friends.

But this particular Remembrance Day, I was at my friend Sean's, who was still serving in the army. I was looking in the mirror, tying my tie and pinning on my medals ready to go on parade. The TV was on in the background, showing the news about other Remembrance parades in London and around the country. Suddenly, I heard the TV presenter announce a news story: 'Bomb blast kills twenty people in Mogadishu.' This in itself was no surprise, bomb blasts are regular occurrences in Mogadishu, but this story was accompanied by a grainy black-and-white photo of a face I half recognised and I did a double take, thinking, 'Oh my God, I know that face. Where do I know that face from?' And then I turned round from the mirror, looked fully at the screen, had a little moment, stared at it again and realised with dismay that it was Abdifatah from the Sahafi Hotel. It was a horrible moment and a lot to take in on a day of remembrance.

Unknown to Abdi, his warning to me had turned out to be a warning to himself. I felt wretched for him as I stood proudly on parade later that morning. I'll never forget his kindness towards me, his advice and his generous and sincere hospitality. He was a true gentleman with a strong code of honour and a deep concern for his people and his country. If it wasn't for him, I doubt I would have ever gone on to run in the beautiful Somaliland.

CHAPTER ELEVEN

AN UNDISCOVERED BEAUTY

During my short trip to Hargeisa, in Somaliland, I learned a fascinating history lesson. This was a long way from the Mogadishu I'd left behind, not only in air miles and distance but also from a social, economic and justice perspective too.

According to the international community, Somaliland does not exist at all, which, after visiting it, I find incredibly sad. You won't find this place on many tourist maps. Somaliland is an unrecognised self-declared state, determined to be independent and separate from Somalia. It is home to millions of people with its own ruler, army, police force, democracy, postage stamps, currency, and even has its own flag – but it's still not recognised as a 'proper' country by the rest of the world, making it extremely difficult for Somaliland to attract aid, investment or tourists.

On 18 May 1991, Somaliland quietly – and mostly unnoticed by the rest of the world – announced its secession from the rest of Somalia. This unilateral declaration of independence was triggered by the overthrow of President Mohamed Siad Barre, the military dictator who oversaw Somalia's gradual deterioration from disintegrating democracy to crushing totalitarian regime, civil war and anarchy.

Post-secession, the contrasts between the two parts of the Somali Republic are vast. Somalia is still locked in a complex and unfathomable civil war that has claimed the lives of over 300,00 civilians, while Somaliland is relatively peaceful and a bastion of democracy, good governance and non-sectarianism. However, on 18 May 2011, Somaliland celebrated its twentieth anniversary of independence, sadly still unrecognised by the rest of the world.

Despite its persuasive legal case for recognition as an independent country, the international community still treat Somaliland as a rogue breakaway state, its sovereignty is unrecognised by neither the United Nations, the African Union, the International Monetary Fund, the World Bank, the Olympic Committee, FIFA, nor, even more ignobly, by its former protector, Britain. It remains legally attached to Somalia with its tragic moniker as the 'most dangerous place in the world'.

Today, Somaliland is a constitutional multi-party democracy headed up by a President, a Vice-President and a

Cabinet, with presidential elections held every five years. Its economy is unstable and mainly agricultural, which relies on plentiful rainfall, a problem in the drought-ridden Horn of Africa. Some of the biggest contributors to the Somaliland economy are those Somalilanders who live and work abroad and send large amounts of money back to their homeland annually.

There is one cause that unites all Somalilanders and that is their desire for international recognition, but the problem is that the African Union doesn't look kindly on any secession movements. International recognition would bring boundless advantages to the region. Somaliland would be able to borrow money from the IMF and the World Bank. It would be able to advance its basic services such as electricity, gas and water supplies, not to mention funding for schools, colleges and hospitals. Any positive media exposure linked to international recognition would deliver much-needed interest from potential investors and tourists. This planned 10k race, open to all Somalilanders and any interested foreigners, was one way of opening up the country and bringing awareness of the nation to the outside world.

True to his word, James Willcox from Untamed Borders had gone out of his way and smoothed my journey into Somaliland. He also arranged a place for me to stay in Hargeisa. After the let-down that was Mogadishu, I was pumped up and ready to run 10k in Hargeisa. But first I had to check in with James. I thought it wise to let him know of the risk of me potentially having an epileptic seizure mid-run, although I was feeling right as rain and had been for some time. I signed all the documentation and disclaimers saying I was responsible for my own insurance and stuff, but still James was unsure. 'Bloody hell, Jordan, you sure about this?' he asked.

'No worries, it'll be fine,' I replied, handing him one of my EpiPens – just in case.

James had arranged another fixer for me. This one was a right character named Shabella and his job was to show me around a bit. I wanted to see the touristy things, hang out a bit with a few of the locals and visit some of the kids in the many orphanages scattered around the countryside. Shabella was a skinny, elderly guy, more like a tour guide than security. He'd lived in Somaliland all his life and knew everyone – including the local police and the military. His phone rang about every thirty seconds with people wanting advice or questions answered. He was extremely knowledgeable about local history and gave a lot of historical tours for foreign journalists. He was a great ambassador for Somaliland and very proud to show me all the different bits of society. Even things that were relatively unimpressive to me, like minor cultural artefacts or a strategically placed flower garden, meant a lot to him. He saw any visitor as an opportunity to share his voice and take it to the rest of the world. If I told him I wanted to do something, he didn't mess about – he made it happen.

'I kind of want to do something a bit different, a bit off the beaten track while I'm here. Can you take me to any of the orphanages around here?' I asked.

'Yes, sir, there are many here and it will be my pleasure to escort you, but first I must show you something very special. Something we are very proud of, that speaks of our heritage. You will like it, you'll see.'

Having returned to the UK then flown back out, I had three or four free days before the run and was keen to crack a feel of the local culture, so I was happy for Shabella to take me anywhere he thought might interest me, but I wanted to get my fill of Hargeisa before I ventured further afield. Hargeisa is Somaliland's largest city, though it still doesn't feel quite big enough to be called one, and is more like a low-rise dustbowl. There is no embassy, no airline and, refreshingly, not a whisper of a Burger King or a Barclays Bank in sight. There was no evidence of five-star hotels, no traffic lights, no billboards, no museums, theatres, cinemas and no swanky office blocks. There was not a sniff of cosmopolitan air to be had, nor any comforting features whatsoever. But its simplicity nurtured a certain charm. Its pragmatism was endearing and what you saw was definitely what you got. The remains of a MIG fighter jet which had crashed during an aerial bombardment of the town was particularly moving, situated as the centrepiece of the town's war memorial.

The place was full of shacks and huts amid dust-strewn streets. It looked rather like someone had chucked a load of Lego on the ground to see how it would construct itself. The haphazardness of the architecture was compensated for by the brightly coloured exteriors. Hargeisa was a vivid place, even down to the brightly coloured fabrics the women wore, so different to what I was to see women wearing in Afghanistan where the dress code is far more strict and the women are expected to cover themselves from head-to-toe in burqas.

The street corners were studded with men chewing and spitting wads of green khat, a native plant of the Horn of Africa. Khat contains the alkaloid cathinone, which is a stimulant said to cause excitement, loss of appetite and a mild sense of euphoria – a bit like a three-shot cappuccino. As the men hung lazily around street corners, scores of women, dressed in long, bright chadors and khimars in various shades of red, pink and blue, hurried along gathering dates, fruits and vegetables from the sprawling Hargeisa market. Occasionally they would have to dodge young men on mopeds as they sped through the market before finding a suitable place to stop and sell that day's supply of khat. The noise of car horns and shouting from the street vendors selling their wares was deafening, but after a while I got used to it and stopped noticing the racket.

The labyrinth of stalls sold everything from fruit and vegetables to slabs of raw meat, packaged food, fabrics and electronic goods. Donkey carts jostled for space on the dusty roads, dodging the odd camel and goat which had wandered away from the local camel market. Overwhelmingly friendly and practically crime-free, the streets of Hargeisa felt more like an extension of the local countryside rather than a serious urban conglomeration. Because of the collapse in the currency, street vendors exchanged literal bricks of bank notes, piled up in carts and wheelbarrows as though they were simply hawking corn on the cob. These barrows were the local equivalent of our high-street banks back in the UK. Entire barrows stacked with Somaliland shillings were more or less worthless.

'If you want to buy Somali currency, you will have to lug more than fifty kilos of notes in exchange for only ten dollars. It will not surprise me if our currency disappears soon as the central bank does not manage the financial system well,' said Shabella.

'Hardly worth the bother,' I said. 'People are literally trucking pocket money around in wheelbarrows.'

Now it was time to for Shabella to let loose. I could see he was champing at the bit to show me this 'magical' place he'd mentioned. We got in the car and travelled the road to Berbera, turning left onto a rough, un-signposted track until we came to a police roadblock. From there it was another 1.5 km drive until we reached a place called Laas Geel and my mind simply got blown away.

It felt incredibly eerie to emerge from brown fields where nomads grazed their livestock and drive down a dry, sandy track, to be faced with the most glorious and elaborate rock art. We clambered out of the car to face panels of ancient cave paintings executed somewhere between 9,000 and 3,000 years BC. The rock art at Laas Geel, meaning 'source of water for camels', is believed to be the oldest and best preserved of its type in Africa. I saw about a dozen painted shelters scattered on a gigantic outcrop of granite. The paintings have been preserved where they stand due to their sheltered location and the dry Somali climate. I was amazed that the colours remained so vibrant, a timely reminder of the country's pastoral lifestyle thousands of years before it reached western Europe. Here, right in front of my eyes, was proof of Somaliland's rich heritage. It was in total contrast to the travail and horrors of years of civil war and I felt the remnants of any lingering depression and stress fall away.

The Laas Geel caves were discovered by a French team of archaeologists in 2002 and are now part of the most compelling tourist site in East Africa, topping anything UNESCO World Heritage could offer. A mixture of black, white and colour representations of animals and humans flickered on the cave walls. I couldn't work out what the humpless animals were – certainly not camels, probably cattle of some sort. They were painted in profile, tottering on two legs with huge swinging udders underneath and horns shaped like lyres with decorations hung around their necks. Stylised human figures with tiny heads adorned with crowns and carrying spears popped up everywhere. They were accompanied by hunting dogs and were pictured dancing among the cows, antelopes, goats and giraffes. I thought of Evie and wished she could experience this amazing sight with me. She would have loved it. She and I spent many hours together making arts and crafts back at our home in Andover.

One day, Shabella took me to visit the cultural centre in Hargeisa to see a dancing show put on by local boys and girls. It was more like a drama class which included dance and music. I was invited to join in and dance, so I hopped around for a bit from one foot to the other, trying to keep in time to the music and not lose my balance. I noticed some of the girls tittering behind their hands. I didn't take offence. In fact, it made me smile – I'm a big bloke and can be a bit clumsy. It was a brilliant afternoon and I was more than happy to be the cause of much amusement.

I also got to take part in a women's basketball game, again in the cultural centre. I was the only man in the match, obviously, but this time my height came in handy for dunking the ball in the net. These women were really good basketball players and fully embraced me being in their game. They were high-fiving and clapping and running circles round me. They were fast and unexpectedly aggressive! I can't imagine what they must have thought of this great lump of an Englishman lumbering about the court.

The contrast between the violence of Somalia and the relative peace of Somaliland was remarkable. At no stage did I feel threatened and I asked Shabella why it was necessary to have an armed guard here. He reminded me of the killing of a British couple who worked as teachers in Somaliland, shot dead by unidentified gunmen back in 2003. Dick and Enid Eyeington were killed as they watched television at their home in Sheikh, over 700 miles north of Mogadishu. Although there was no obvious motive for the killings, aid workers in the region informed me that they believed the couple were probably victims of Muslim extremists. I couldn't help but think about the number of murders in London, especially the spate of recent stabbings which trumped that lone double murder big time. So far, Somaliland had only shown me peaceful, smiling, friendly people willing to go the extra mile to help strangers. I was looking forward to getting started on the big run the following day, meeting more locals and immersing myself in the fabric of this wonderful place.

CHAPTER TWELVE

IRONY

The day before the race in Hargeisa, I had to go to the Ministry of Sport to register. The place was heaving with local people keen to join the race. I met two excited guys from Hargeisa, named Ali and Mustafa, who told me they had been busy training for their first run ever. They were sure they could beat me, I loved their calm confidence – I didn't doubt them either, but I didn't let on. All the runners were buoyed up and straining at the leash. They could hardly contain themselves, but we still had one full day to go…

It amused me that every second person I met in Hargeisa claimed to be a cousin of the Somali-born runner, Sir Mo Farah. They all wanted to talk about him and because I lived in England, asked if I knew him. People were incredibly friendly. Although they seemed quite surprised to see a white

Western face, they were genuine and open, with seemingly no ulterior motives. One day, while walking with Shabella in the local market, an elderly local woman approached me saying, 'Oh, mister, mister, come…' Her husband was standing right beside her and, being aware that it was not culturally acceptable to make direct eye contact with Muslim women, I tried to ignore her. I tried to remember all the things the military had taught me and attempted a polite acknowledgement with a nod of my head and tried to walk on by. But she carried on, 'Mister, mister…' in a bid to attract my attention.

'No, no, it's OK, you can go and talk with her,' said Shabella.

'I don't know, I don't want to offend anybody by doing the wrong thing.'

'No need to worry – this is Somaliland. You can speak to anyone here.'

So I went over to her and I shook the husband's hand first and put my hand on my chest in greeting. 'A pleasure to meet you,' I said. I was quite surprised when the woman thrust her hand out directly to shake mine. I looked at her husband for permission to shake his wife's hand. He responded with a smile and invited both Shabella and me inside their home for a cup of chai.

Their house was a simple shack with a mud floor. A fire blazed in the centre of the room over which a large pot hung, brewing tea. Neither of them spoke English, so Shabella became our interpreter. They asked what I was up to and what I thought of Somaliland. They were telling me places where I should go and what to see. The following day, they told me, was the camel market, and amusingly, the woman explained how I could buy my own camel. I tried to make a joke of it, telling her I lived in England and the camel wouldn't fit on the plane home, but the joke kind of got lost in translation. Then the husband got involved in the conversation, telling his wife that it would be cheating if I rode the camel in the race the following day. The whole thing was quite surreal. Imagine a total stranger in Blighty inviting you into their house for a cuppa – it just wouldn't happen, and if by chance it did, you'd be worried they wanted something you weren't prepared to give.

Being a Muslim country, I was fascinated by the relationship between men and women in Somaliland. I read that Somaliland is one of the least visited countries in the world, so the interaction between males and females and the way that females acted with tourists, visitors and guests like me was not what I expected. It felt unusual to have so many women stopping to speak to me in the street. If I were to walk through London, I don't think many women would stop to say hello out of the blue, and especially not Muslim women. It would be against their protocol and beliefs, but I found the women in Somaliland very open-minded and happy to talk and to engage – even to the point of inviting me into their home for tea. The rest of the world could take some valuable lessons from Somaliland and its warm, kind and welcoming people.

That night, back at my accommodation, thinking about the day's activities and the race ahead, I had a bit of a panic attack. I thought, shit, what if I do actually have a seizure? It was so bloody hot here, all I could remember was the doctor telling me the heat and the stress on my body could trigger a massive seizure. I'm in the bloody middle of a foreign country that the rest of the world chooses not to even acknowledge exists, where hospitals and healthcare aren't the best. No one's going to come and bail me out if I start frothing and foaming at the mouth. I heeded my trainer's advice to take on plenty of fluids, checking I had several bottles of water with me and reminding myself that it wasn't about winning the race, it was about getting to the finish line in one piece and raising aware-ness for epilepsy as well as children on the front line.

The race itself started and finished in the National Stadi-um in Hargeisa which was a proper football stadium with a football pitch in the middle and a running track around the outside. There was a lot of media interest in both the event, being the first mixed-gender 10k race in Somaliland, and in me personally. I was a bit of an oddity – the English guy from the UK who was bonkers enough to be running three races in three of the most challenging and complex places in the world. The BBC World News was reporting as well as local media, who were keen to show the outside world that Somaliland was a very different place to Somalia. Their message to the rest of the world was: 'Look how safe we are, we're having our own international race and foreigners are keen to get in on the act. We can't be that bad after all.' I probably spent about half a day in all doing interviews with the press and the local media who were interested in me and why I was there. The people distinctly differentiate themselves from Somalia and I sort of played up to that quite a lot with the local media, truthfully telling them that I found Somaliland so warm and welcoming and that I hoped they would eventually get the recognition they sought.

There were a few other international runners taking part, one from Romania, two from Italy and one runner from Canada along with several others. Some of them were serious runners; they probably had a thing for dark tourism and a desire for adventure in weird and wonderful places. This was certainly one of them. Everyone was busy tweeting, sharing and posting to social media. The local Somalilanders were proud as punch that foreigners were coming for a 'holiday' to run in their race. The atmosphere was electric. There was a real buzz in the air and a full-on party vibe. Traditional African drumming music was playing, people were dancing and the place was bustling with journalists, local media and loads of excited teenagers and young men and women all trying to sign up for the race. They obviously loved it that a Westerner was chatting to them. It was not a normal occurrence and for some I was the first Westerner they had seen. The Minister of Sports was there and again he was very welcoming, shaking my hand and thanking me for coming to his country. The whole atmosphere captivated not just the runners, but the families of the runners. People everywhere wanted to get involved in this momentous occasion, even if they were just standing at the side of the road waving a Somaliland flag.

I walked down the tunnel where the players come out on match days and into the changing rooms. A prayer mat lay on the ground in the corner and a poster of football tactics was pinned on the board. I took the opportunity to have a bit of quiet time, just thinking of the race ahead and what it meant to me to be able to take part with the other 200 runners involved.

As soon as the starting gun sounded, the locals, obviously inexperienced in distance running, were up and out there going hell for leather. No pacing for them, so it wasn't long before they were all huffing and puffing, trying to catch their breath and clutching their sides. I was more cautious, taking it slow and steady.

It was an exhilarating experience running alongside female counterparts in a Muslim country. It wasn't anything too common in my experience, but for lots of people seeing a husband and wife running alongside one another is pretty unheard of. The women sensibly paced themselves, while the men sprinted ahead trying to be superheroes. What really made me chuckle though, was that every time a female runner looked to be on the verge of overtaking a male runner, the guy would speed up. Some of the women runners were even elbowed off the road by the guys. Male pride was at stake here and it wouldn't look good to be beaten by a woman!

It must have been so damn hot for those poor women running dressed in long skirts and hijabs. It was hot and deathly humid, but you can't be exposing your bare skin as a white Western male, so I had to join the women and wear full cover – long black sleeves and black running leggings. The Somaliland men seemed able to get away with just wearing T-shirts and shorts.

I wasn't concerned by running fast, which was definitely not my usual philosophy on winning. In this case, it was the taking part that counted for me. There was a collective atmosphere of joy and it wasn't hard to be caught up with it. To have the kids running beside me was the icing on the cake. I find if you're concentrating on just running, running, running, you don't get to enjoy it or absorb what's going on around you. It was great to run through the villages, to see the people, to high-five the kids and locals at the side of the road, to even stop sometimes at the water stations and have a chat with other runners.

One young Somaliland boy, who must have been about

sixteen or seventeen, named Alou, latched on to me and wanted to run alongside me for the whole race. I became his pacemaker, urging him on. As we ran he tried to tell me about his family, his brothers and sisters and his life as a schoolboy in Hargeisa. His broken English made him difficult to understand and it was hard for him to get the words out in between his breathlessness. We were encouraging each other to just keep going like proper running buddies. Every so often he would give me a strangled look and say, 'I've had enough. I can't keep going. I'm ready to stop.' But I didn't want to encourage him to throw in the towel, so I kept stopping to go back to him and pull him along with me. Although he was unaware of it, he was helping me get through it all as much as I was helping him.

We crossed the finishing line together about an hour later, back at the same starting point at the National Stadium. The crowds cheered us wildly, jumping up and down and gleefully waving their national flags. Every once in a while a kind stranger would thrust a bottle of water into my sweaty palm. It was the most incredible experience, made even better by finishing alongside a Somaliland local. Alou thanked me for not giving up on him and encouraging him to push on through. My new-found running buddy was quite shocked that he'd actually managed to complete the race; after the first half-hour of running he never expected to. To be honest, neither did I.

I felt a rush of adrenaline and pride as I stood on the podium to receive my medal, along with the other race participants. It now sits in pride of place on my office desk back at home in Andover, between old football trophies and a photograph of my daughter.

One thing I did learn on this run was to be more sensitive about the Somali flag. I was carrying the expedition Running Dangerously flag which included the Somali flag (along with Iraq and Afghanistan), but here I was running in Somaliland. Perhaps it was not the best idea to pull insignia out for photos that included the Somali flag when I finished the race. I learned later that a couple of people had frowned upon my actions and so I went to visit them to apologise. On reflection, this was an important lesson on cultural sensitivity – an obvious one, too – and I guess I got a bit caught up in the moment for which I apologise to anyone else who may have taken offence in any way.

Unfortunately, one of the over-keen Somaliland runners was unable to complete the race. The heat and pressure got to him and he collapsed before he reached the finishing line. He was carted off to hospital. James, the race organiser, and I went to see him back at his home the following day to check he was OK. Even though he was unable to finish the race, we presented him with his medal for sheer guts and endurance. He was rather embarrassed to receive it in front of his entire family, but I reckon he was seriously chuffed too. A lot of the local runners had sprinted, thinking it was the done thing in a marathon. Perhaps next year they'll remember to pace themselves. And although the terrain wasn't easy, it was designed for maximum participation and maximum completion, with just a few inclines for the runners to battle against. The race is now an annual event and it will be great fun to see how it develops and how the race creates awareness of Somaliland and international recognition for its bid for independence.

Sport is one of those things that brings people together of all backgrounds and cultures, ages, races and genders. It's magically unifying. For the Somalilanders, this race was a massive development. It was their way of announcing to the world that they were a peaceful community. Although there was an obvious military and police presence, with the odd police and ambulance siren screaming in the background, the place wasn't crawling with them. And even though my expedition was called Running Dangerously, it was ironic really, because at no time in Somaliland did I ever feel I was in danger. In fact, it was quite the opposite. All things considered, it was a pretty conservative place. After all the stress, not being able to run in Somalia had worked out all right in the end. It's a funny old world, isn't it?

CHAPTER THIRTEEN

THE ULTIMATE VICTIMS
OF WAR

It appears that many world leaders today are failing to protect children deliberately targeted in war. Children living in war zones have come under direct attack, including being used as human shields, killed, injured and recruited to fight. In countries like the Democratic Republic of Congo, Yemen and Nigeria, rape, forced marriage and abduction have all become standard tactics. In Afghanistan, children make up the majority of all civilian casualties and fatalities and, sadly, schools and hospitals in Yemen have come under frequent attack and been used for military purposes, thereby denying children access to healthcare and education. War and malnutrition is a massive killer of children in Yemen.

In Somalia, several thousand children have been recruited by armed groups and thousands more have been taken from their homes, leaving families devastated. More countries are at war now than at any time in the last thirty years. For too long terrorists and insurgents have been committing atrocities with near-total impunity and it's only getting worse. Children living through conflict are among the least likely to be guaranteed their rights and much more can and must be done to protect them. In my view, relatively small amounts of money can make an enormous difference to children on the front line and can go a long way to changing their lives. As I travelled through Somalia and Somaliland, it became clear to me how important it is for us to go out of our way to assist these desperately needy kids and the fragile aims of the charities and volunteers helping them.

After the race was completed and all the excitement of the run had dissipated, I took the oportunity to visit a few more of the orphanages in Somaliland with my guide. I spoke to people in my local network and was told where and how to find some of these out-of-the-way orphanages. I wanted to see beyond the work of the larger charities like UNICEF and Save the Children and see what was really happening at grassroots level out of the cities and towns. These orphanages, I knew, would have very little funding and be totally reliant on volunteers and the goodwill of the local people.

After the grotty orphanage I visited in Mogadishu, I found some of the smaller orphanages in Hargeisa more tolerable.

Some of them still looked like prison compounds or basic military establishments, with the walls topped with razor wire, for example, but it was easier to judge the better ones from the dire ones by the smiling faces of the children. I was fortunate to see some better ones where the children were happily running around, playing football. Some of those kids reckoned they were the next Cristiano Ronaldo or Lionel Messi, as they kicked and tackled, passed and headed and practised their keepie-uppies. They loved it when I joined in and taught them a few footie 'tricks'. Their footballs, however, were either made up of rolled-up sweaters or half-deflated bits of rubber, so I went into the local town and bought ten brand new footballs for them to kick about. They were thrilled, but I remember watching a young lad who was still very much emotionally attached to his deflated ball and who continued to kick it around the compound, completely ignoring the new bouncy balls the other kids were playing with.

The orphanages were mixed gender and the girls loved the ball sports just as much as the boys. We played basketball, catch, football, really anything that involved a ball. The simplicity of their games and the joy the children took in playing was delightful to watch. Some of the kids spoke to me in broken English, as did some of the volunteers working in the orphanage, but mostly the kids and I communicated through hand signals and just kicking the ball about.

I managed to have a look inside the orphanage and a chance to check out the living and sleeping areas. It was none too clean, a bit grubby, in all honesty, and not very hygienic, but they did their best with the little they had. One of the orphanages I visited was run by a British charity called SOS Children's Villages. It was made up of thirteen family houses, housing 130 children, a community house, a village director house, administration buildings, a service house/workshop/ store and a multipurpose hall and a 'tukul' (an African hut). This hut was a classic round shape with a thatched conical roof and made of mud, grass, millet stalks and wooden poles. The kindergarten was a smaller area accommodating four group rooms, including one hands-on for children with special needs and a kitchen. The family social centre provides help to hundreds of children a year and focuses on the formation of community support groups, whose members exchange information and experiences and support each other emotionally. They also create awareness on the prevention of HIV/Aids in the community and lobby for protection of orphaned and vulnerable children. I was particularly interested in the fact they provide books, school uniforms and school material to pupils and lobby the government to provide bursaries. At the same time, the charity helps Somalilanders to obtain loans, skills training and equipment based on individual family needs for income-generating activities.

Twenty-four hours after checking to see I was indeed who

I said I was and not some weird guy off the street, I had the privilege of visiting the orphanage. I was pleased to note they put adequate security measures in place and at no time was I left alone with any of the children. The place was well organised from what I could see and the children looked remarkably happy. There were eight kids to each 'home' and each home had a 'mother', who was assisted by a female volunteer the children called 'sister'. 'Mother' and 'sister' were responsible for running the homes, keeping things in good order and teaching the kids basic lessons such as reading, writing, maths, cooking and sewing. The concept worked well and the kids were obviously cheerful, referring to their voluntary mother as 'Mama'.

One of the little girls in the orphanage took a bit of a shine to me. Her name was Rayan and she looked to be about four years old. An immediate rush of memories of my own little girl at that same age flooded my mind and I felt very tender towards her. She was a shy little thing who hung back from the crowd of other kids, mostly boys, who were all jostling me, eager to talk and get my attention. When they all rushed off to play football, she remained where she was, smiling shyly at me. I went over to her; we made contact via goofy smiles and high-fives and bonded over a skipping rope. I didn't want to alarm her or frighten her, so I made a bit of an idiot of myself, pretending to trip up and fall over my own two big feet. Eventually, she came out of her shell and began to laugh with me.

I was really touched when she asked her house mother if she could be the one to show me her accommodation in the orphanage. She was very proud of her little home. It was something that belonged to her; her sleeping space was something she could take personal ownership of. We all trooped inside with Rayan clutching my hand tightly and a lump forming in my throat. She had nothing really. There was no sign of any toys, just a wooden bunk bed with some simple bedding and a wardrobe with shared clothing hung inside. But it was all clean and tidy and these kids were obviously living in a safe, happy and loving environment.

The house manager told me Rayan's sad little story. Her mother only lived 300 yards down the road in an area for the homeless, but she had abandoned Rayan when she was just a few days old, leaving her on the steps of the orphanage. Her mother was destitute and believed her daughter would have a far better life being cared for in the orphanage where there was electric light, water, food, a comfortable place to sleep, lessons to learn and friends to make. One of the locals told me the heart-breaking fact that Rayan had no idea where her mother was, or that she actually comes once a week and waits silently outside the orphanage gate hoping to get a glimpse of her daughter and ask after her welfare.

I felt so affected by Rayan and her sad story that I asked whether I would be able to sponsor her and provide some funds for her care and education until she turns sixteen.

Every few months I receive a photograph and an update of her progress. My own daughter, Evie, knows all about Rayan and I hope that when Rayan is old enough and able to write herself, I can link them both up as pen friends.

Having completed the race in one piece and managed to get through without suffering either a seizure or a hostage situation, I felt a massive sense of relief. It was an amazing feeling getting on that plane to travel back to the UK. I was euphoric – I had done it. I was full of gratitude for my life with my family and my daughter. My depression and anxiety was beginning to lift and I could see a bright future ahead. Travelling, adventures, getting involved, raising money, running, meeting people and learning about their lives and their personal challenges had been liberating. I was aware of having achieved lots of interesting and exciting things in my life before, but many of them had been tinged with a hint of anxiety. At no time had I actually felt this fulfilled. The sense of community that running with others provides and the support and social elements of running with others was invaluable. I felt in a good place mentally, physically and emotionally. I was determined to make this an annual trip and keep in touch with the wonderful new people I had met. The first run of three was over but I still had the excitement, the thrills and the adventure of two more to come. Now it was all hands to the pump to get ready for the run in Iraq – a place that held many dark memories of my time serving there.

CHAPTER FOURTEEN

BACK TO IRAQ

The pain was intense – my thighs were cramping, my breath heaved raggedly in my throat as, with maximum effort, I put one foot in front of the other. Head forward, arms pumping, I slowly chugged along. Only four miserable miles into this Baghdad half marathon and I'd hit a brick wall already. The severe temperature had sapped all my energy. So much heat was retained in the tarmac and the concrete that my quads were sizzling. The flaming inferno in my legs was killing me and I wasn't sure how much more of this I could take…

• • •

Iraq was a country I knew well, having served in the military here back in 2005 and 2007. It was also a place that held heart-breaking memories for me as a serving British soldier. I had lost several of my friends here in conflict situations.

They call Iraq the 'land between two rivers'. A civilisation built on the Tigris and the Euphrates, the country is made up of the snow-clad mountains in the north, the desert and the sandy, flat plains in the southeastern lowlands. The history of Iraq has been one of conflict and bloodshed, but in between those moments of horror have been times of splendid sophistication and culture. It was Iraq, after all, who gave the world the number zero in mathematics. It's the land where writing first began and where the stories of *One Thousand and One Nights* were first told. It was the home of the Hanging Gardens of Babylon and the mythical Tower of Babel plus the likely location of the biblical Garden of Eden.

The twentieth century brought war to Iraq, the Iran–Iraq war and the Iraqi invasion of Kuwait ushering in chaos and disruption. Saddam Hussein's totalitarian regime resulted in major suffering for the Iraqi people who were subjected to stringent economic sanctions by the United Nations. Corruption at this time was rampant, with the crime rate soaring, a massive fall in living standards and a huge rise in diseases and infant mortality rates. It's been estimated that the brutality of the Saddam Hussein regime killed more than three million of his own people. Things got even worse when the US-led coalition toppled Hussein in 2003. There was no better future for the Iraqis as expected – just years of sectarianism, insurgency and misery, as much of the money allocated by the US for rebuilding programmes had to be funnelled into security measures.

When the US occupying forces began to leave Iraq in 2007, Iraqi rule was reestablished with free elections. But nobody foresaw the devastating effects of the rise of ISIS and the subsequent collapse of the Iraqi forces. Like the government, the local population were shocked at the emergence of ISIS and vast numbers of Iraqis have since fled the destruction and atrocities caused by them.

ISIS, also known as 'Islamic State of Iraq and the Levant' (ISIL) and 'Islamic State' (IS) or 'Daesh', originally started as an al-Qaeda splinter group. Their aim is to create an Islamic State, or caliphate, across Iraq, Syria and beyond. Their desire is to implement Sharia law, which is rooted in eighth-century Islam, and to establish a society that mirrors the region's ancient past. They are a truly evil and barbaric organisation, known for killing dozens of people at a time and carrying out public executions, crucifixions and other extreme acts of violence. They are also clever sods, using modern communication tools like social media to promote their reactionary politics and religious fundamentalism. Their fighters actively destroy holy sites and valuable national antiquities in a manic bid to propagate a return to the early days and practices of Islam.

Their revenue comes mainly from oil production, smuggling, taxes, ransoms from kidnappings, selling stolen artefacts, extortion and the controlling of crops.

In 2014, ISIS controlled more than 34,000 square miles in Syria and Iraq, from the Mediterranean coast to south of Baghdad. By the end of 2016, ISIS territory had shrunk to about 23,000 square miles. ISIS was believed to be holding several thousand people as slaves. These unfortunate people consisted mainly of Yazidi women and children, but some were from other ethnic and religious minority communities.

I particularly wanted to run in Iraq in memory of my old friend and comrade, Lance Corporal Alan 'Bracks' Brackenbury, who had been killed in Iraq on 29 May 2005. He and I had been troopers together in the King's Royal Hussars and were promoted on the same day. I can remember having a pint together straight after work after picking up our first stripe as lance corporals; our career trajectory had been very similar. My intention was to commemorate his life by running on the same date as his death thirteen years later with his name proudly displayed on the back of my running shirt. It was a way to remember him and pay my respects, something I try to do every year since we lost him. I was also running in memory of the guys I was on patrol with on 16 July 2005 in Al Amarah, who also paid the ultimate sacrifice for their country – Second Lieutenant Richard Shearer, Private Leon Spicer and Private Phillip Hewett, all of 1st Battalion, The Staffordshire

Regiment, who each died of injuries sustained in hostile action that day. Then of course there was my mate, Sergeant Wayne Rees, from The Queen's Royal Lancers, who also died in Iraq. He had been an army football teammate of mine; he was a great bloke who brought the best of changing-room banter to every game, home and away. And Lance Corporal Paul Farrelly, from The Queen's Dragoon Guards, a good friend who had been through army training with me, who tragically left two young daughters behind; he was awarded 'Best Recruit' in training and was someone who I always looked up to. I had also lost my friend from Blackpool, Gunner Lee Thornton, from 58 Battery, 12th Regiment Royal Artillery. I used to go to Blackpool football matches with him back in the day and I'm still good friends with Thorny's parents, Karen and Mick. All these guys were the epitome of professional soldiers – diligent, motivated, enthusiastic, fit and selfless. These were all great guys who gave their lives for Queen and country and I felt incredibly proud to be able to run in their memory. As well as these men, I have many friends with long-term injuries, psychological wounds and limbs missing. I was running for them all – and of course the children of this war-torn country who were now the main focus of all my efforts.

The half marathon in Baghdad was to be the second stop on my Running Dangerously tour, but just before travelling, I was alerted that the race had been called off owing to the threat posed by active members of ISIS. My first emotion was frustration. This was a major setback. After a lot of graft and hard work I'd managed to attract a good level of sponsorship and funding for this leg of the expedition. Promises had been made to various sponsors and donors and now the whole thing looked like becoming a major fuck-up. I was rightly fed up and worried about how I was going to manage this latest upset.

Getting to the start line for launching the Running Dangerously project had been dependent on attracting the right sort of sponsorship and expertise. Most sponsors donated tangibles like flights, insurance and logistics. Adequate insurance was particularly difficult to secure. If you wander into a norman insurance agent's and say, 'I'm an ex-soldier and I want to run through the most dangerous and hostile countries on the planet, will you insure me?' they look at you like you're either stupid or nuts because you're a massive target for any terrorist organisation. It's an unnecessary risk that nobody's forcing you to take on. It's not like you're delivering aid, or you're providing a service. You're intentionally choosing to go and put your own life at risk and to potentially put other people's lives at risk too, especially if you get into trouble and they have to come to the rescue. Not everyone saw Running Dangerously in a great light. Maybe 95 per cent of people say, 'It's a great thing you're trying to do, pushing the boundaries of human, physical and mental endurance.' But you also get a handful of people who will say, 'Well actually, it's reckless; it's stupid and you're going to end up in a boilersuit on Al Jazeera'.

But my answer is that nothing great was ever achieved in life without taking some risks, and the bigger the risk, the greater the reward. If it's risky for me to go and run through these countries, think about the children who have to live there every day of their lives. I believe we have a duty to help. It's all too easy to sit behind our laptops in our bedrooms playing at being keyboard commandos. More of us need to get off our arses and put something good back into the world.

I was very lucky to have the HELP insurance scheme (Hostile Environment Liability Protection). They very kindly jumped on the project in the early stages and I later presented them with a signed picture of me finishing the Afghanistan marathon with their logo on my shirt. An organisation called Inmarsat provided me with a satellite phone for emergency communications (it turned out traditional mobile phone networks don't work in a lot of these countries because the relevant infrastructure is lacking).

I'm honoured to be an ambassador for Bremont watches, these people are like a second family to me. Their strapline is 'tested beyond endurance' and they involve all these people from whom I take inspiration. These are ambassadors and friends who go and do weird and wonderful expeditions from trekking across Antarctica to winning Olympic gold medals. Bremont are very supportive of veterans and the military and they do a lot of work for charities. I am extremely proud to be associated with them. Ultimately, they were interested in me wearing the Bremont S500 model in order to test it through war and conflict zones in extreme environments. I later auctioned off the watch at the end of the project for charity. I'm pleased to say it raised over £5,000.

The notion of time is important to me, which I guess is why my relationship with Bremont is something I value immensely. We can never buy more of it and it will run out one day. We never know when our own time's up, especially if we're soldiering in a war zone. Time is the most valuable resource in the world, and a great leveller of humanity. The people I met in Africa would say to me, 'The problem with you people in the West is you have all the watches, but we have all the time.' Their way of doing business was slow and lethargic. They're often late for meetings and I would often use that well-known saying, 'Time and tide wait for no man'.

Today, Baghdad is considered one of the world's worst cities to live in. Residents are forced to deal with near-daily attacks, shortages of electricity and clean water, poor sewerage and drainage systems, rampant corruption, regular gridlock, high unemployment and myriad other problems. Ubiquitous checkpoints, concrete blast walls and security forces pepper the city, making it look bleak and unwelcoming. It's nigh-on impossible to get a visa to visit Iraq on your own volition. But because there was going to be an official half marathon and I was intending to compete, I had a justifiable reason to apply for a visa to travel. Now with the race being cancelled, all this was in jeopardy – I no longer had a legitimate reason. So it was back to the drawing board for me. I made a ton of enquiries, but frustratingly, they all led down a dead-end and came to nothing. My trip to Iraq was looking less and less likely and I was beginning to feel despondent.

I put an SOS status out on social media saying I was looking to run a half marathon in Iraq, but it had been cancelled and was there anyone out there in my network who could help my dream come true? It was a massive cry for help and I wasn't really holding out much hope, so I was thrilled when I got five or six responses from privateers and active military guys in Iraq saying they might be able to do something to help.

Then, out of the blue, I got a message from one of my former colleagues, a former officer in my old regiment named Marcus d'Apice. I never actually got to meet him during my time in service, but we shared the same network and he'd got wind of the story of the expedition. By chance he now happened to be the managing director of a large, highly reputable British security company out in Iraq called Control Risks. He reached out and said, 'Jordan, I've been following your journey in Somalia. I know you've had difficulty getting out to Iraq, but I'm willing to put my neck on the line and try and help you if I can.'

Marcus had experienced the challenges of a war zone first-hand, so he totally got what I was intending to do and couldn't have been more supportive. He understood the people of Iraq and knew the terrain I would be running in. He was also the father of two beautiful daughters, so any project that helped give children a better life was close to his heart. I explained my wish to honour my mate, Bracks, and because he'd been in the same regiment, Marcus said, 'Let's do this thing. Just sort out your flights and we'll take care of everything from the moment you arrive till the moment you leave.'

True to his word, Marcus organised my visa and sorted out all the logistics. My stop-over flight from Istanbul was delayed and it eventually took me two days to reach Iraq. By the time I arrived at Baghdad airport, I hadn't slept for over twenty-four hours and I was braindead.

I was met at the airport by the Control Risks security team and escorted to their compound via three armoured Toyota B6 Land Cruisers. The guys were professional and diligent, giving me a security brief before I got in the vehicle. 'Jordan, if we're ambushed at any stage, this is what I need you to do, follow my instructions.' They showed me where the medical kit was, they showed me where the breakdown emergency kit was and we went through all the possible outcomes of our vehicle being compromised or attacked in the forty-five minutes it would take to get me to the compound. It gave me more confidence that they knew exactly what they were doing. They were slick and well drilled. I was listening in on the radio and could hear them talking between vehicles, giving each other what we call 'sitreps' or situation reports, where they update their movements to their command station every time we pass through a checkpoint. They saw me as a client and were constantly checking that I was OK. They were everything that I would want in a professional security detail.

We travelled along Route Irish, a high-profile main supply route. This road is notorious for having been the most dangerous road in Iraq for many years, especially from 2003 to 2007. Many Americans, coalition-forces troops and private contractors have been killed on Route Irish over the past fifteen years. It's the main road between the US Embassy and Baghdad Airport.

It was still only 7.30 a.m. and already about thirty-seven degrees, and the day was only going to get hotter. The compound came into view, four high walls topped with razor wire and armed guards on the gate. But as soon as I entered, the environment changed completely. It was very different to what I'd experienced as a soldier serving in Iraq. It was a very relaxed environment, very slick and very clean, but everything was ready to move at a moment's notice. All the armoured vehicles were lined up, with all the kit and equipment at the ready next to them. If something happened you could see that everyone could grab the essentials, jump in the vehicles and get out of there. There was a ton of British ex-military guys swarming around, instantly recognisable with their short hair and tattoos. Quite a few of them had served in the Parachute Regiment and were hanging out in their Oakley shades with their guns on display, muscled up to the eyeballs. They were looking at me like, 'Who the hell is this guy?' There I was in my running gear, completely out of place, but they were all actually very supportive of what I was there to do.

There was a good-sized swimming pool and a cook house with a full menu and a 24-hour chef service. There were several massive American double fridges stocked with cans of Coke and milkshakes, all the stuff that you would never have got working in the military. You could just help yourself whenever you wanted, no restrictions. It wasn't exactly five star, but considering it was in the middle of Iraq, I would have been quite comfortable living there for some time. It was clear this was designed for comfort and obviously a private-sector set-up. In the military, I had to share a tent with twelve other people cheek by jowl. Here, you had your own private en-suite room. It even had a TV in it!

The guys working at the compound would mainly be escorting private clients, typically they were engineers for reconstruction projects in Iraq, oil or gas workers or energy consultants. Some clients might be senior military generals who are visiting military sites. Private security contractors take a lot of the pressure off military operations by working in areas such as convoy protection and logistics. It costs a lot of money to hire these guys – it's a risky job, but they obviously get paid good money. These guys probably earn in three or four days what I was earning in a month as a soldier.

I was looking forward to resting up, making myself comfortable, having a bite to eat and a kip, but as soon as I set foot in the compound, I was told, 'No time for that, Jordan. We've already marked out the route for you. You have to run today because we've got the guys on the security shifts sorted.'

It was five o'clock in the afternoon. I'd had no sleep and no time to acclimatise to the punishing heat. It was over forty-five degrees out there by this point and already the sweat was pooling under my arms and running down my back. A 13.1-mile run loomed ahead, beckoning like a witch's claw. My heart sunk to the bottom of my trainers. I grabbed a quick bite to eat, just enough to give me a boost of energy, and off I set, already exhausted, for one of the most gruelling experiences of my life.

Marcus had arranged for an armed vehicle with a camera to follow me on the run, clear the route and head off any trouble. Once again, I was anxious about having a seizure mid-route and I gave the former British special forces medic who was sitting upfront with the driver an EpiPen and instructions on how to use it – just in case. Mostly, the security vehicle stayed 100 metres behind me, but every fifty minutes or so, it would take off for ten minutes, scoping out any potential danger ahead. Having a seizure during those ten minutes was not worth thinking about.

As I ran, I was surprised just how much heat was retained in the tarmac. I hadn't fully appreciated how hot the ground would get and how much of that heat would be transferred through my whole body. I'd done a few training sessions back in the UK with Olympic athlete and European silver medallist Chris Thompson, and as the burning intensified I remembered his advice to me to pour cold water over my scorching quads as well as over my head, neck and chest area. I was wearing a hat with a sort of flappy neck protector, so gave that a good dousing every so often. That wet hat was a life-saver.

Only four miles into the run and I hit the feared wall I'd been warned about. I was having trouble breathing and I was sweating buckets. Every so often I'd have to wipe the sweat from my eyes as it stung so much. My whole body felt like it was cramping up. My legs were humming with pain and my vision was beginning to blur. The road ahead began to wobble and take on a fuzzy kind of glow. This was madness, I'd only run for four measly miles. I prayed to whatever god was listening not to let me fall down and give up. I'd definitely underestimated this run; it was a lot tougher than I thought it would be. If I felt like this after four relatively flat Baghdad miles, how the hell did I think I was going to manage running a full marathon of just over 26.2 miles in the arduous mountains and high altitude of Afghanistan?

As I slogged on, I eventually passed the pain barrier and got into a steady rhythm. This was the toughest thing I had ever done either physically or mentally. I forced myself to just keep going, driving myself forward. It was hard to feel motivated, running on my own without the camaraderie of other runners as I'd experienced in Somaliland. There was no one to slap you on the back to keep you going and no shared words of encouragement.

When I first set off on the run, I was wearing a small waist belt in which I carried my running gels full of electrolytes and a few bottles of water, but after four or five miles I ditched the belt because its weight was putting a strain on my back and slowing me down. Thankfully, the guys in the van following me kept chucking me the odd bottle of water so I could take a rehydrating swig. Eventually, a set of mighty blisters built up on the back of my heels. I could feel the skin ripping away from my skin and sticking to my socks. But the pain from the blisters was minuscule in comparison to the pain of the heat from the tarmac road scorching the underside of my feet.

At first the streets seemed eerily quiet. But as I ran on, I began to see more evidence of people going about their everyday business. I ran past plenty of soldiers and police at checkpoints, all of them armed. I ran past a couple of manned tanks at the side of the road. I had a British flag sewn on to the front and back of my vest, so they knew I was a mad English-man. They gave me a wave and a few looks of puzzlement that obviously meant, 'What the hell is this crazy guy doing?' All the time I was thinking, 'Bloody hell, I'm fucking dying here.'

The thought of raising money for the kids had pushed me forwards in Hargeisa. Here in Baghdad it was the war memorials to the fallen that kept me going. There were scores of memorials and commemorations scattered along the roadside and although they were a sad sight to see, they were also a motivating factor. I took the time to rest up and look at the writing on them as I passed. Etched into the metal slats and concrete podiums, some of which were quite artistically and creatively designed, were lists of the names of British, US and Iraqi soldiers who had been killed on active duty. They were well preserved by the local community and the sentiment and message touched me deeply.

The run through the streets of Baghdad was full of memories of my time serving in Iraq. As well as the thoughts and recollections of my friend, Bracks, the burnt-out cars on the side of the road were powerful reminders of my own experiences of conflict. The streets were humming with tanks and soldiers carrying guns. It was a familiar scene and it was the thought of running for my mates and former colleagues who had been killed that kept me putting one painful foot in front of the other.

The final mile of the run was an absolute killer. I thought the end would never come as the last mile of sand stretched ominously in front of me. But the end of the run itself was strange. Because it wasn't formally organised and was just a solo event, there were no crowds to greet me. Neither were there any people to wave flags or cheer for me. There were no onlookers to chuck bottles of water at me and there was no medal to pin on and no winner's T-shirt to wear, but when I crossed the eventual finish, I felt a massive sense of accomplishment at achieving the run in one piece.

Later, I went to visit the Monument of the Unknown Soldier in central Baghdad. The monument was built by Italian architect Marcello D'Olivo and completed in 1982. It's dedicated to the martyrs of the Iran–Iraq War and represents a traditional shield dropping from the grasp of an Iraqi warrior. It was originally built to help instil a feeling of national pride, while also immortalising Saddam Hussein's reputation as a powerful leader. It looks like a massive copper dome, quite an awe-inspiring sight. Under the shield was a cube made up of seven layers of metal to represent the seven levels of Heaven in the Islamic faith. Inside the layers I could see sheets of red acrylic which were supposed to represent the blood of slain Iraqi soldiers.

I'd wanted to visit a few schools while I was in Iraq to see if there was any help we could offer or any supplies we could buy. It was important for me to try and formulate some sort of relationship with schools, because obviously a big part of my work was access to education. But, unfortunately, it was actually quite difficult to find schools I could visit. I drove past several that were now just derelict buildings. There were clearly signs to show they were once education establishments, but they were now riddled with bullet holes from the war. Visiting proved to be problematic. I was reliant on the organisers from Control Risks and I didn't want to abuse their hospitality or take the chance of putting anyone else in danger or compromise their lives with my wanderings. I wouldn't have been able to live with myself if anything kicked off, or if a dangerous incident occurred in a high-risk area as a result of me wanting to wander off to see a school.

Before the first Gulf War, Iraq had an educational system that was one of the best in the region and was free of illiteracy, but the governments that came after the occupation have neglected education. I didn't want to push my luck, but I did get to visit one Iraqi school about a half-hour drive northeast of Baghdad. I made contact with the principal before we visited with the plan that when I got there I would teach a short English lesson to the kids. But when I arrived a day later I found a very controlled environment. They obviously put on a bit of a show for me, but it all felt like I was there to do a school inspection. It had an air of visiting royalty at an army camp, totally inauthentic. The classroom was tidied up and all the kids were sitting nicely in rows with their legs and arms folded and big grins on their faces. I was only shown around certain pre-planned areas and was forbidden from deviating from their plan. Although it was a very orchestrated visit I did get to interact with some of the kids. However, I wasn't allowed to take any photographs, which is often the case when children are involved. Even though I was speaking to the principal and staff through an interpreter, they were quite evasive when I tried to ask questions relating to how the children coped with living through the troubles that Iraq had seen over the last two decades. They sort of brushed over my questions by trying to change the subject, saying, 'Oh, we must show you our new selection of books.'

When I visit schools, I take everything that's told to me by the managers or the staff with a pinch of salt because of course they want me to see the perfect environment, but I always make a better judgement by looking at the children and seeing how they're behaving and if they are they smiling, or if their environment looks conducive to learning. If this lot weren't truly happy then they were very well disciplined.

Until fairly recently, Iraq was considered *the* most danger-ous country in the world. So many young men were being killed daily that it was said they took to having a small symbol tattooed on their bodies in case their faces were mutilated beyond recognition and they were unable to be identified. But, after the defeat of ISIS, the people of Baghdad are slowly readjusting to the possibility of a life with less violence and death. One of the Iraqi interpreters back at the security com-pound said, 'We are trying to take things slowly because in our country, there is always something to be afraid of.' I could see evidence of a hint of optimism. On my run I noticed a few cranes indicating new builds, a few newish-looking clothes shops and shopping malls and a couple of restaurants. I also noticed quite a lot of young men hanging around the streets, seemingly with jack all to do. There aren't many jobs around and the best ones are in the army or the police, and these are all taken. But it was heartening to see Baghdad returning to some sort of normality in which staying alive wasn't the first thing on everyone's minds.

'I understand you would like to visit an orphanage while you're here,' said the interpreter. 'I'm not sure we can accommodate you here on this trip, but let me tell you a little about the state of our orphanages here in Iraq. They are a mess.'

'Tell me more…'

'The children orphaned in battle with ISIS have become our forgotten casualties. Unlike the government soldiers who fought these battles and who are honoured with memorials in nearly every town, Iraq has no resources for these victims. Despite what you see, our country's ravaged communities are still scrambling to build basic services like healthcare and electricity. They are too overwhelmed to manage the needs of orphans. Many of these orphans are the children of ISIS fighters and they are stigmatised and abused for that fact. In Iraqi orphanages you'll find the ways that war wreaks its destruction, embodied in the most innocent of faces. You will find children of those killed, children born of rape, children who have been abandoned in the chaos of battle and children of the enemy, many of whom are the sons and daughters of foreign jihadis who came to join the Islamic State group and are now either dead or incarcerated.'

'Surely, no child is responsible for his parent's actions?' I replied, 'Each child is a victim. Each child needs love.'

'You are quite right, but I have heard the most terrible stories of children who were found in a dreadful state. One baby was so thirsty she died in the hospital a few days later. She had no energy left to live. Others were found abandoned in the streets after being left out in the sun as bait to draw Iraqi soldiers into the direct line of fire. Some were apparently found in the destroyed and abandoned homes after their parents died fighting with IS.'

It sounded highly doubtful that I would get to visit one of these orphanages without putting a lot of people out, so I reluctantly gave up on that idea. But, to this day, I'm grateful for all the help I got in arranging the Iraq leg of the expedition. I was looked after by the very best guys who did all the risk assessments and organised all my security details. It was a top-notch, professional job, which concluded with a terrific donation to our charity. Best of all, I'd managed to stay upright. I'd not had the seizure the docs were so worried about. My energy and stamina were improving, my head was clearing and the anxiety that had always dogged me was beginning to lift. The big test would be Afghanistan. I'd be doubling up the miles, running in adverse, mountainous terrain in stupid heat and high altitude with limited security. Was my mental health and my physical stamina up to it?

To up my game and prepare for Afghanistan, I decided to take part in the Great North Run in Newcastle, a half marathon of 13.1 miles which I ran for Epilepsy Action. The Great North Run is the largest half marathon in the world and takes place every year in September where participants run between Newcastle upon Tyne and South Shields. The run was first devised by former Olympic 10,000-metre bronze medallist and BBC Sport commentator, Brendan Foster, I had the pleasure to meet him on the day and it was clear to see why so many people were in awe of him. Brendan had a huge personality and was a real lively character with positive energy in abundance, and having him share some words of motivation with me at the start of the race was a welcome honour.

I was thrilled to see Kelly Holmes actually at the start line waving to me and shouting, 'Good luck, Jordan!' I remember she was recovering from a painful back injury that day, but she was there as an ambassador for sport, going around cheering for everyone and shaking their hands. To see Dame Kelly at the start line gave me that extra bit of boost. 'Bloody hell,' I thought, 'I'm standing next to a double Olympic champion here, this is serious stuff.' It ended up as a terrific run with a carnival vibe and spectators handing out bottles of water and throwing jelly babies at runners as they passed by. However, I didn't find it easy by any stretch of the imagination. In fact, it was bloody hard, but I really tried to block everything else out and concentrate on just putting one foot in front of the other.

I also ran in the Winchester half marathon. There's a jewellers in Winchester, called Burrells, who had kindly offered to sponsor the Afghanistan leg of the project and I thought it would be a nice touch to run in the Winchester half marathon because my sponsors were from that city. Unfortunately, I didn't realise the race was run over the hilly South Downs. I'd assumed it was just running around the pavements in the city. So again, that was a challenge. I was quite surprised how many hills there were so early on in the race. The second half was relatively flat, but I was so fatigued by that point, it felt like I was still running uphill anyway. I was thinking, how the hell am I going to do double this in Afghanistan when I can't even cope with running a half marathon on a nice cool day in Blighty? But I knew a lot of it comes down to psychological resilience. I knew that as long as my mind controlled my body and not the other way around, I could run all day if I needed to. The moment I let my body say to my mind, 'I'm done, I'm finishing,' there would be no turning back. It's really the simplest process ever to just keep pushing forward. It's the same with life; you will have challenges, you will have hurdles to scale, but as long as you keep moving forward, you will always get to where you need to get to in the end. Whether you're running a marathon or just plugging along in life, keep moving forward and don't dwell on what's behind you because it's been and gone. Take the lessons. Keep moving. Keep attacking. Always.

CHAPTER FIFTEEN

THE LAND OF THE TALIBAN

I'm not one of those people who says, 'I have no regrets in life', because I would be lying. I have many regrets, but what's important to me is that I always continue to push ahead, take the lessons from the mistakes I've made and apply them to my future. I would always encourage anyone to chase their dreams if they want to achieve something, but most importantly they have to believe and be prepared to make the sacrifices to get there. I think it's also important to realise that nothing great ever happens alone. I've surrounded myself with good, positive people who are full of energy and value the things that are important in life, especially family and loved ones. It's too easy to get tunnel vision and forget those around you when you're on a mission, and I'm sorry to say I learned this the hard way. But completing the runs in both Somaliland and Iraq had set something off inside me. I could feel my heart lifting at the thought of moving on into Afghan-istan and completing the final run of the expedition.

Although my depression was still dogging me, I could feel it slowly lifting as my days looked brighter and my motivation grew. I've always believed that if we can help people less fortu-nate than us, we should do so – in fact, I believe it's our duty as human beings. I also believe that by helping others we help ourselves without even realising it. As far as I'm concerned, I think there's too much talking in life and not enough action. There are those that talk about it and those that 'do' some-thing about it. I try to be in the latter group when I can. My daughter, Evie, will always be my greatest achievement in life and no award, expedition or materialistic gain will ever top this; she is my pride and joy and the love of my life. I run for her as much as I run to raise money for helping children on the front line. It's Evie who spurs me on and keeps me going when the black dog comes yapping at my heels and I'm emo-tionally or physically exhausted.

People have asked me what my daughter thinks of me doing stupidly dangerous activities and whether it's fair on her, but she has bags of courage and is learning to look fear in the face. In 2017, we were in Florida together and Evie announced that she wanted to swim with dolphins. She had seen it on the television and it all looked so tranquil and peaceful; she was dead keen to give it a go, but I knew in the face of the real thing she would be scared. We got in the water, all kitted up in the snorkelling gear, when all of a sudden this creature about three times the size of Evie sidles up to her and she starts to cry and shake with nerves. 'What's up with you, Evie?' I asked.

'I don't think I want to do this now, Dad,' she said.

The idea was that she was going to hold on to the dolphin's top fin and the dolphin was going to swim around, but in all honesty I think she was petrified by it, even though the dolphin was really quite friendly and disciplined. In the end, she managed to conquer her fear and get on with it. I think she just needed a little nudge and I was rewarded by a brilliant smile of pride in her achievement.

Afterwards we went to the café and had a piece of cake and a drink together. We talked about how she felt about facing her initial fear of the dolphin. 'You know, Evie, you went from being a nervous little girl who was petrified of being with the dolphin to being the dolphin's best friend and wanting to take it home. I'm really proud of you.'

'Yes, but I was scared at first, Daddy.'

'Maybe you weren't scared, maybe you were just really excited. Have you thought about that? Sometimes when we do things that scare us a little bit, we learn to overcome our fear and that is when we grow and learn new things.'

I explained how, as humans, our brain and our body is designed to protect us from anything that's a bit scary, anything that's risky, anything that's a bit dangerous, and because it does that it limits our growth sometimes. It limits our ability to develop as people because we're too busy worrying about something going wrong. I suggested that maybe we should try and think differently and start thinking, what if I did do it after all and it all works out well and actually this dolphin takes me for a swim and we have the best time ever? 'There are going to be lots of times in your life, Evie, where you will be uncomfortable, but if you start to think of it differently you might also have some of the best experiences you ever have in your life.'

Unbowed by the fatherly lecture, Evie asked, 'Do you get scared when you go running in these war places, Daddy?'

'Yes, these are places where people have died or where people have lost people they love. Of course, I'm nervous, and a little bit scared, but I'm also excited because these are places where not many people in the world have been to. The children there can't swim with dolphins; they might never see a dolphin in their whole lives. They will never have the privilege like you of swimming with these beautiful animals. But I want to go out there and hear their stories because these children have special stories to tell too. It's just that their stories are very different from yours or mine.'

After successfully completing the Iraqi leg of the expedition, I was now facing my biggest physical challenge. If running in Iraq had taught me one thing, it was that I was going to have to get a whole lot fitter if I was going to run and finish my first ever full marathon. I'd had the benefit of some welcome support in Somaliland and Iraq from the guys at Untamed Borders and Control Risks but now I would be running 26.2 miles in the tortuous heat, dust and altitude of Afghanistan. I'd enjoyed company and comradeship along the way, but now I would be running with no buddies, and no personal security detail. Yes, I was apprehensive, but I was also excited and gagging to get started on the final leg of this current adventure.

Afghanistan is a landlocked country between the Near East and Indo-Asia and is at the heart of Asia, traditionally part of the Greater Middle East region. It's bordered by Pakistan to the south and east, Iran to the west and Turkmenistan, Uzbekistan and Tajikistan to the north. To the far northeast is a short border with China but the terrain there is mostly remote and inaccessible. Afghanistan has been devastated by countless wars during the last forty years, and as civil war took hold of the country in the mid-1990s, the Taliban emerged. The Taliban are a Sunni Islamic fundamentalist political movement and political organisation whose aim is to impose its interpretation of Sharia law in Afghanistan and remove foreign influence from the country. The Taliban's project as a political force was to halt the civil war and bring some semblance of order to the shattered country. They were backed by foreign money and enthused by a conservative set of Islamic rules and mores. They soon captured the capital of Kabul, and by the year 2000 they controlled most of the country apart from some areas in the northeast. The Taliban were condemned internationally for their harsh enforcement of Islamic Sharia law which resulted in the brutal treatment of many Afghans, especially women. As well as becoming a force for terror in the country, they also engaged in cultural genocide, destroying numerous historical monuments.

Afghanistan is still suffering from the conflicts of the past two decades and is still technically a war zone, hence visiting is extremely dangerous. The government retains little control over much of the country and terrorism is a huge problem, with government forces kept busy fighting Taliban insurgents. Sadly, the country suffers from rampant corruption, grinding poverty and opium cultivation. Landmines and other unexploded ordnance remain a problem across the country, killing or maiming many hundreds of civilians a year. I knew I'd have to stick to well-worn paths rubbed raw by the countless footsteps of people before me and also make sure I avoided any red and white painted rocks warning of unexploded mines. The beauty of the Afghan landscape belies its danger; it's all too easy to forget that the country is a conflict zone and not a play area. For me, the risk was worth taking to spend time in this extraordinary and beguiling place.

Afghanistan was obviously the big one for me and I was only too aware that I'd never run a marathon before. I'm sure a lot of people thought running my first ever marathon in a war zone was a pretty crazy thing to do. I know my mum was proud of me and my achievements, but she was also concerned for my safety. But one of the things I wanted to do was to challenge people's perceptions about Afghanistan because it's also an incredibly beautiful country if you look beyond the bombs and bullets. Like Iraq and Somalia, there's a lot of incredible stories of humanity and of people doing small things for the greater good of the world.

I knew Afghanistan relatively well from my short time there as a security consultant. A negative Western narrative about the country still litters the mainstream media and affects the way people currently view the country. Before my journey out there, I was asked to speak at a private fundraising dinner event in London, where the Afghan ambassador would be in attendance. As I stood at the podium, I made a joke that the place was full of challenges from the outset. Getting a visa to travel was difficult at the best of times, but one of the pros of visiting Afghanistan was that when I was waiting at the visa queue, I noticed the line was relatively short. I told the audience that I had remarked on it to the man queuing next to me, who quipped, 'That's 'cause nobody in their right mind wants to visit as a tourist.'

After my talk, the Afghanistan ambassador to the UK came up to me with his blessing and some kind words. He was supportive of what we were trying to achieve. One of his jobs as ambassador was to shine a positive light on his country and to help attract funding for further development and education.

Naturally, he was keen for us to create awareness of the worthy side of Afghanistan; it wasn't all doom and gloom. Later, he kindly sent me a few video messages personally wishing me luck in the marathon.

• • •

When I eventually arrived in Kabul, the capital of Afghanistan, the organisers of the marathon told me there had been several recent serious security incidents. Two suicide bombs had exploded that very week, the first one killing fifteen people, the second one killing twenty-three. This was another blow to my plans because I was in Kabul when I needed to be in Bamiyan Province, over 100 miles away. Because of the security threat, the airline I was intending to travel with had decided to terminate all their flights. The flight time wasn't too long, only about an hour, but now I faced a new quandary. My previous two trips had thrown up some sort of spanner, why should this one be any different? How was I going to get myself to Bamiyan? I thought, 'Bloody hell, what are we going to do? I've got all the way here.' I was desperately thinking of contingencies I could put into place… Maybe I could go to my friends in the military out there and run a marathon in their secure compound, or maybe they could help me find an alternative route. When I put it to them in panic mode, they were all welcoming, 'Yeah, 'course, Jord, we'll help you if you need us to,' they offered. But that wasn't what I was there for. I wanted to run in the marathon of Afghanistan, the official marathon, not some back yard out in the arse end of nowhere on my Jack Jones, nor indeed in some secret compound.

When I approached the organiser of the marathon about my concerns, he told me he was working on it. I decided to put my faith in him and hope he was as good as his word. After a bit of minor angst on my part, we decided to put in an application to get on a United Nations flight due to fly out to Bamiyan Province. We put a solid case together, saying we were a charitable project trying to raise money for educational projects in Afghanistan. We were rewarded with, 'Yeah, no problem, if we have a spare seat you're welcome to it.' Result! But then they also told us we would have to fly out the very next day. There was no time to waste owing to their own tight schedule. Unfortunately, there was no guarantee of a scheduled flight back again, but that was a risk I was prepared to take. So far, everything had worked out well, even when our plans had gone to pot.

So, that's how I ended up on a little twelve-seater United Nations flight. Me, the organiser, a Norwegian runner, a couple of local Afghan runners, a journalist covering the marathon, a couple of UN workers providing aid and an American adventure athlete who was pursuing his dream of being selected for the US Olympic team and was heading out to Afghanistan to train for the trials. We were also accompanied by a UN worker specialising in unexploded ordnance who was there to assess the amount of unexploded bombs in the area. The South African pilot had a really good sense of humour and did a little brief tongue-in-cheek talk at the start of the flight. 'Welcome to the UN flight service,' he said. 'For those of you joining us on your honeymoon in Afghanistan, a double welcome. I hope you get to enjoy the magnificent beaches, but please do remember that unfortunately, there will be no alcohol served on this flight.'

The plane itself was not designed for comfort as it usually flew humanitarian aid workers moving around the country. The seats were narrow and hard as rock, but the journey itself was incredible. The views over the mountains were magnificent. They looked like something from the Discovery Channel. It was hard to believe that the country had been at war for so many years because the landscape was like something out of the world's best adventure brochure. The mountains below me were covered in several different layers of green and brown and were topped with snow caps. The beauty of the landscape belied its true nature. It was odd to think the mountains below still held Taliban strongholds with fighters living there. It was far too easy to let my guard down and relax until I remembered the plane intentionally flew at a certain altitude to dodge the surface-to-air missiles, which was common practice as I remembered from my time in the military.

I've always considered Afghanistan to be a country of rare beauty and majesty, and its geology is fascinating. Millions of years ago massive shifts in the underlying tectonic plate resulted in the formation of elongated blocks of mountains and deep valleys. The sheering, deposition and erosion of the rock has continued ever since. Today, you can see that two major faults cut through the mountainous area of the Hindu Kush. The Chaman fault runs from the Arabian sea to Kabul, while the Hari Rod fault crosses northern Iran and runs up the Hari Rod Valley until it forms the valleys of Bamiyan and Ghorband. But what really amazed me about the country's landscape were the astounding features left by the retreating glaciers. In their place remain boulders and rock, sand and grains, all pushed into incredibly distorted shapes and patterns throughout Afghanistan's deep valleys. In between the fault lines lie blocks of land that were once islands, now squeezed and distorted by the pressure of continental collisions. I was intrigued to learn that the pressure on these blocks are responsible for the many deadly earthquakes that plague eastern Iran, Afghanistan, Tajikistan and Pakistan. Around 5,000 earthquakes occur every year in Afghanistan, 500 of which are serious enough to register on global seismic networks. It's a country that's constantly rocking and rolling.

The rain and snow from the Hindu Kush pours down thousands of gullies and ravines, creating magical lakes full of diverse nature and waterfowl and the region's tectonics produce geothermal springs and chemical deposits of bril-liant colour. Some of these lakes shine a bright blue, which is the result of sunlight reflected in the particles of glacial silt. The Afghanis have a word for this silt – 'khaki', because of its colour. The silt gets blown in the strong winds and finds its way into every crevice and fold of your clothing. The khaki is also a component of Afghan soil which is so rich that the people only have to add water to grow fertile fields of barley, wheat, cotton, flax, sesame, tomatoes, peppers, fruits and potatoes. I found that one of the more intriguing aspects of the landscape is that it's sometimes difficult to see the dif-ference between natural features and those made by humans. Rocky overhangs become natural caves, crevices become strange-looking staircases, perfectly rounded hills sit on top of perfectly flattened plains. The remains of old settle-ments are a gloomy sight as they lie dusty, ruined and aban-doned. What weirded me out was that the iron in the rocks, south of Bamiyan, give the impression of blood at sunset. Sometimes a row of landmine craters appears in the blood-red rock at semi-regular intervals, a timely reminder of the horrors of war.

It wasn't just the beauty and the magnificent geology of the landscape of Afghanistan that drew me back. My former work there resulted in a handful of friends left still working in the country as security contractors or military guys who were still in the army. When they heard of my plan to stay in one of the local bed-and-breakfast hotels, they were insistent I stay with them. 'You can't stay in a B&B downtown. Are you mental, Jord?' they asked. 'Why don't you stay with us?' They lived in secure camps and compounds, but I really didn't want to stay there. I wanted to be at the forefront of Afghan life. I wanted to embed myself with the locals and embrace their way of living. Also, hanging out in an armed military compound was another double-edged sword, because these compounds were the first port of call for any attacks by the Taliban.

I wanted to keep as low a profile as possible. I'd already grown a pride-worthy beard before my journey out to Kabul and I chose to wear the traditional garb of the shalwar kameez, a long, white, knee-length shirt over a pair of beige baggy trousers. Bloody comfortable it was too! Easy to wash daily and very necessary as the Afghan dust finds a way into all your bodily creases. Bamiyan Province was to Kabul a bit like Somaliland was to Somalia for me. It was the most incredible, hospitable place. I felt no fear of the locals, many of whom went out of their way to help me. I was able to safely and freely walk around the town with no personal security. I had been warned that there was still unexploded ordnance in the area and I came across a couple of empty ammunition cases just lying around on the ground too, but they were extremely weathered and clearly from times gone by. Apparently, these are quite common – marks of the past and a reminder of war left lying around in the streets. I spent a few days in Bamiyan before the marathon, getting acclimatised to the weather, the environment and the people.

The harm inflicted by three decades of war on the people and the country of Afghanistan has been cumulative. The total population of children killed is not known, but considering that half of the population are under the age of twenty, we can reasonably assume it's a pretty large number. The hazards of war have resulted in maimed bodies and missing limbs. Many of the children on the streets have been victims of landmines. Children, like the general population, have also been subject to dangerous radiation through ground and aerial attacks where uranium bombs and shells have been used. I had heard that cluster bombs designed to look like food containers had also been picked up by starving children with the inevitable consequences. Afghanistan is a deeply devout Muslim culture and as well as the displacement and maimed bodies of the children, the most striking aspect is the lack of women on the streets. Most of the places I went to like the restaurants and cafés were full of men, with not a woman in sight. Many of the women remained at home in traditional roles, cooking and caring for their families, hidden away from prying eyes. The Taliban are known for their sexism, misogyny and violence against women. Their motive is to create an environment where the chastity and dignity of women is sacrosanct. When the Taliban were in control of most of Afghanistan, Afghan women were forced to wear the burqa at all times in public.

One of the English-speaking men I got chatting to over a cup of chai in a market café told me that the women used to have to cover their faces because the Taliban believed female faces were the source of corruption for men not related to them. 'Things have improved a lot since the fall of the Taliban,' he told me, 'but in the old days women were subject to harsh restrictions. They could not go out in the streets at all if unaccompanied by a male relative. If they were allowed to speak, they had to speak quietly and not raise their voices and they were absolutely forbidden to laugh in public. They were not even allowed to stand outside on their own balconies, or go to any public gatherings. And high heels were outlawed too, in case their footsteps excited a man.'

I wasn't surprised, I knew he was only giving me half the story of the terrible restrictions women had to endure under Taliban rule. Their lives were bloody horrific. I knew for a start that a girl's education stopped at the age of eight and that was if they were lucky enough to even have some basic schooling. This was so they could work in the family home and prepare for marriage – usually to a much older man. I also knew that many of them hid away in clandestine schools in other Afghan women's houses. News about these secret schools would spread by word of mouth, woman-to-woman. I'd heard stories about young girls hiding their schoolbooks and pencils under their burqas. It was all secret and hidden under pain of death. If any of the women involved in the teaching were caught they would be persecuted, jailed and tortured.

Following decades of conflict, Afghanistan has focused on revitalising social systems to protect and care for Afghan women and their children, but the challenges remain and day-to-day life can be daunting. Most Afghans live in rural districts and lack access to basic services. The majority of them have grown up surrounded by conflict and this has affected their access to education, healthcare, clean water and sanitation. I was surprised to learn that a fifth of Afghan children die before their first birthday and that many are unable to reach their full mental or physical development because they suffer from acute malnutrition and their drinking water is contaminated with faecal matter. Although the Taliban no longer held power, Afghanistan is still a deeply patriarchal society. Men rule and women still have very little control over their lives and their education, I'm afraid to say. Forced marriage is still extremely common, with men making all the decisions over women's minds and bodies. In some rural areas of Afghanistan, young women are even bartered in family arrangements, essentially becoming slaves. Ariana Television, the largest private media channel in Afghanistan, reported that children were sold for food by their families in the north during the 2007 drought. They are put to work at very young ages in the fields, or work on the city streets where they are at risk of exploitation, poor health, severe injury and even death. As a result of these conditions, Afghan children suffer from one of the highest mortality rates in the world. They are the tragic victims of war in a society whose support systems are weak or non-existent. This is a society where the traditional networking and customs which once offered protection have all but broken down. Peace is ultimately necessary for the long and arduous task of rescuing Afghanistan's children from their tragic plight.

One of the first trips I made was to visit the remains of the Buddhas of Bamiyan. My guide was a truly lovely man named Ali Shah. His English was impeccable. Ali hoped to be the first man the Afghans ever sent to the Winter Olympics; he was a skier. He absolutely loved the sport and although he didn't qualify, he was still invited as a guest to represent Afghanistan. He told me tales of how relentless his struggle to obtain funding had been. 'Most people,' he said, 'get the opportunity to train in places like Switzerland and Austria, but I had to do all my training in the Afghan mountains with limited resources and hardly any equipment.' I noticed that even the jacket he was wearing was all ripped and damaged, but he was very proud of the Olympic rings on it and the Afghan ski team logo. Ali was a knowledgeable and passionate man who I still consider a friend today, and with whom I still talk and share a lot of photos online.

Originally, the two Buddhas of Bamiyan were sixth-century monumental statues. They were massive statues carved into the side of a cliff high in the Bamiyan valley in the Hazarajat region of central Afghanistan. Both of these sandstone sculptures originally depicted Buddhas with serene faces, their bodies swathed in carved folds of sandstone 'fabric'. The larger statue was originally painted red, the smaller was multi coloured. But what I saw in front of me now were two giant gaps in the rocks where these Buddhas had once proudly stood. They were dynamited and destroyed by the Taliban on the orders of their leader, Mullah Mohammed Omar, who declared the Buddhas as idols. The Taliban said they were destroyed in order to protest the international aid that was reserved exclusively for maintenance of the statues, while the rest of Afghanistan was experiencing famine.

Afghanistan's radical clerics began a campaign to crack down on 'un-Islamic' segments of Afghan society. The Taliban soon banned all forms of imagery, entertainment and sports, including television, in accordance with what they considered a strict interpretation of Sharia. The destruction of the iconic and ancient Buddhas was seen as cultural vandalism by the international community and an example of the extreme religious intolerance shown by the Taliban.

Before their destruction by the Taliban, these Buddhas were the largest examples of standing Buddha carvings in the world and their destruction became a symbol of oppression and a rallying point for the freedom of religious expression. I found the caves at Bamiyan awe-inspiring. There were innumerable

Me and my former army colleague Rick Webb, who lost his leg in Afghanistan, giving a talk to children.

I was invited in for tea and welcomed by the Somaliland people wherever I went.

Participating in a basketball match in Somaliland. These women are challenging many of the perceptions people have of this part of the world.

LEFT Weekly camel market in Hargeisa, Somaliland.

BELOW The Running Dangerously project attracted significant media interest not only in the UK but in every place I visited, too.

At the start line in the national stadium, Hargeisa, Somaliland.

Celebrating crossing the finish line in the first ever mixed-gender race in Somaliland with two local runners, what an honour!

High five – an international sign of peace and welcome (or something like that!).

My local guide, Shabella, and our armed guard at Laas Geel.

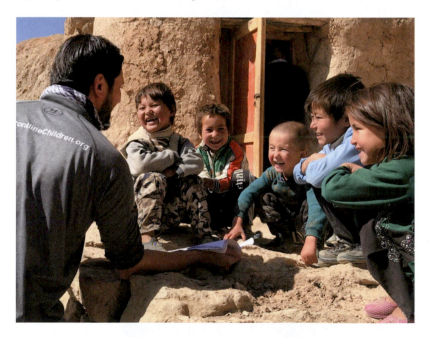

I'm always amazed by the sheer joy expressed in children's faces despite the challenges surrounding them.

An Iraqi girl looks out through a hole in the wall of a school, which is littered with shrapnel from ammunition strikes. © WATHIQ KHUZAIE

ABOVE Speaking to a local soldier in Baghdad about how the current challenges are very different to those on my last visit ten years earlier.

LEFT A main battle tank manned by Iraqi troops in the background as I run through Baghdad.

ABOVE Spending time with the locals and embracing their culture is one of my favourite parts of any adventure.

LEFT A little Afghan girl I met on race day in Bamiyan Province, Afghanistan.

LEFT Crossing the finish line of the marathon of Afghanistan 2018. My first ever marathon was one of the most fulfilling achievements for me personally.

Visiting the British military cemetery in Kabul was a very moving experience, especially seeing the names of friends and former colleagues.

Bamiyan Province, Afghanistan, one of the most beautiful places I've ever visited.

So much natural beauty to be found in Afghanistan, sadly hardly known to the rest of the world.

Teaching English to child refugees in Afghanistan. I love spending time with children; their smiles are always infectious despite the adversity they face.

The Band-e Amir national park in Bamiyan Province is perhaps Afghanistan's best natural beauty – simply breathtaking.

There was a real sense of irony having 'HELP' plastered across my back as I ran through war and conflict zones – even the locals found the funny side.

excavations riddling the hillsides for about eight miles or so. The locals referred to them as 'Soomuch'. The hills were honeycombed with these caves and reminded me of little troglodyte homes or something out of *The Hobbit*. They were nothing fancy – just simple squared-out dwellings cut into the rockface. Some of them were adorned with little carved friezes, others were topped with small domes. It felt and looked other-worldly.

One of the reasons for visiting Afghanistan, apart from running in the marathon, was to seek out some 'off-the-beaten-track' schools. I wanted to see for myself how the local children had been affected by war and how their lack of resources was impacting their education. I asked my guide, Ali, if he knew of any such schools or orphanages he could take me to visit. 'Our education system is problematic,' he said. 'It has been severely disrupted due to the conflict-related violence. Many of our schools continue to close their doors due to direct threats and attacks. It is very worrying. The next generation will be compromised if we cannot protect children's right to education. For many of our children, completing primary school remains a distant dream.'

'Some robust action is urgently needed against those people committing these attacks, don't you think?' I asked.

'Indeed. It's not just threats against schools, it's also hospitals and the people who work in them. Anti-government elements have sent public and private threatening messages

including texted death threats by mobile phone or radio messages criticising vaccination workers. It's all about creating a
climate of fear and intimidation.

Ali told me there had recently been two school burnings,
two improvised explosive device attacks and once incident
of abduction. 'The schools that are here provide lacklustre
education in broken-down buildings. The classrooms are
undersupplied and overcrowded and the teachers are able to
teach only for a few hours before the next shift of students
comes along. The teachers are all well-intentioned, of course,
but some have never even graduated high school themselves.
Being able to educate children safely is one of the most important developments in society. It's one of the most important tools in fighting war, poverty and unemployment. But
come, enough of this – I have a really interesting school to
show you which I'm certain you'll like to see. It's completely
voluntary; they get no funding from international charities or
organisations and,' he paused, 'it's unusual.'

So, Ali and I set off on our journey. It was a bit of a mystery
where we were actually going, so I was quite surprised when
we drove up to the side of a bare mountain with just a little
window cut out in the side and a steep slope leading up to the
entrance. 'Is that it then?' I asked, 'That's the school?'

'Yes, this is it. Come, I'll show you.'

We walked into the cave and I ducked down as we entered;
the ceiling was dangerously low. It was like entering a bizarre

magical kingdom. The whole cave widened into one large room and was kitted out with an array of things visitors had brought for them over the years. There was an old map of the world, dated about 1970, taped to the wall of the cave, its edges brown and curling. There was one shelf with about ten well-thumbed books stacked on it. The covers looked ripped and scribbled on. The shelves were not exactly groaning with reading material and, sadly, the poverty and obvious lack of resources was in stark contrast to any school I'd visited in the UK. The few books they did have were basic easy-reading level, nursery stuff. But one or two were more heavy weight; huge political tomes and some old out-of-date encyclopaedias. There was something horribly incongruous about it all. Sitting on the floor on brightly coloured woven rugs were about thirty smiling children between the ages of roughly five and twelve.

Ali and I were welcomed by the one lone teacher, a lovely lady named Freshta, who also spoke impeccable English. She was a little nervous when we first got there, wringing her hands and fussing around the children, because we were filming and taking photos and there was an obvious risk to her and what she was trying to achieve with the school. Advancing the cause of education for Afghanistan's dispossessed was a dangerous activity and could result in punishment or death. 'I must tell you,' said Freshta, 'many teachers here in Afghanistan, especially female teachers, have been killed, beaten, abducted or threatened by fighters after we have been accused of siding with the government.'

I totally understood her defensiveness, but after I explained the project and the ethos behind Running Dangerously, Freshta couldn't have embraced it more. I was thrilled to have managed to get past both her fear and her scepticism.

Freshta told me that she volunteered her time every day for about three hours to teach the children. Most of these kids were either refugees, homeless or from poor families with deprived backgrounds. She was so passionate about volunteering her time and educating the children. She was a remarkable woman, proud of her little school, devoted to her charges and dedicated to helping the next generation. Although she spoke English, the kids mostly spoke Pashtu, but we all got by with hand signals and a bit of miming. I have the best memory of standing in front of that class of children and teaching them to sing, 'Heads, Shoulders, Knees and Toes'. They all seemed into it, smiling with delight and yelling out, 'heads' or 'toes' at the appropriate moments! Those children were all very well ordered. Each stood and introduced themselves to me stating their name with big grins. Those that could speak a little English, taught to them by Freshta, pointed to the left or to the right, showing me the direction in which they lived.

Freshta was thrilled that we were taking an interest in her cave school and were willing to help with some funds. 'I love your little school, Freshta, but why set it up here?' I asked.

'This is because Afghanistan remains a hotbed of conflict, suicide bombings and airstrikes, and schools are sometimes caught up in the crossfire. Also, armed groups have taken over many of our established schools as barracks to house soldiers or fighters, or as bases to mount security operations. More military use of schools and hospitals means more danger of attack, as well as harm to the children's education. It is out of the way here – and safer. It's not ideal, but it's better than nothing. Nearly half of our children in Afghanistan are out of school due to conflict, poverty, child marriage and, of course, discrimination against girls. All this violence has forced many of our schools to close. It is particularly bad for our girls, many of whom have never even set foot in a classroom before.'

Freshta became rather contemplative, searching for the right words. 'We must not forget our girls,' she continued. 'Most Afghan men will not allow their daughters to be taught by a male teacher and there are not enough female teachers here in Afghanistan. It is a problem for us. So few of our schools are for girls only and most of these lack basic sanitation facilities, which ultimately makes going to school even more unappealing for these girls. Don't forget many of our young women choose or are forced to marry before their fifteenth birthday. It is hopeless for them really.'

Later that day Ali and I went to the local market and bought some books and writing materials, and Ali returned to the cave that night to give them to her along with $100 to spend on any resources she needed. Just before we left, Fresh-ta gave me permission to use any of the footage I had filmed that day of the school. 'I shan't do that if it makes you feel uncomfortable, or if it puts you in a potentially dangerous situation,' I said.

'No, you must make your film,' she replied. 'It is critical for the rest of the world to see the importance of education in Afghanistan. There has been too much fear and division here. We have to keep our children coming to school. When they are not in school, they are at increased danger of abuse, exploitation and recruitment as child soldiers. But a strong education system is key to getting more of our children in school and keeping them there. This is the only way to help them become healthy and responsible citizens.'

As I left that bunch of happy kids, my heart melted to see them all skipping off back into the mountains. They lived in terrible poverty with the barest of essentials, inadequate shelter and the threat of constant danger from insurgents or unexploded ordnance, but what they were not short of was joy, love and respect. It was incredible to witness and I left that little cave school humbled and awash with gratitude for everything I had and all the wonderful people I was blessed to know.

Freshta and I have stayed friends to this day and we have fun exchanging emails and photographs and news about her pupils. I'll be sending over supplies to the cave school with an Afghan runner competing in next year's marathon.

I'm currently planning a competition where her pupils are designing a running T-shirt for school children in the UK. Here in the UK we are holding an Afghanistan mini-marathon fundraiser so that when the Afghanistan Marathon 2019 takes place we will be replicating a one-kilometre race for UK schoolchildren. The Afghan children are designing the T-shirt for the UK children and the UK children are designing T-shirts for the Afghan children.

Back in Bamiyan Province, Ali took me to visit the local market. One of the streets we walked down was called 'Meat Street', for obvious reasons as it turned out. There were carcasses of whole cows hanging on giant meat hooks from stalls set up on the side of the road, their severed heads lined up one by one on plastic sheeting on the ground. The whole street was full of dead animals hanging and the stink was nauseating. Their throats had been pre-slit and the blood left to drain right there in front of you on the ground. It was all done quite openly in the street – bugger the health and safety regs.

It's quite common in these countries to have whole streets that sell the same item, so the streets are named after the item being sold or the service being offered. I walked with Ali down 'Shoe Street' where piles of leather shoes were being sold. They were all tipped straight from the back of a truck into one giant heap on a tarpaulin on the ground. Some of them weren't even in pairs, but it didn't seem to bother the men who bought them. They seemed quite happy to scrabble in the pile of shoes and pick a left one and a right one. So what if they didn't match? Nobody batted an eyelid to see a bloke walk around in odd shoes. They were a comfy pair of shoes, right? Social norms here were very different. One little kid was wearing a really old fake Manchester United top and a pair of Manchester City shorts. You couldn't get away with wearing rival derby teams in the UK, but this kid was dead proud of his football kit.

One of my favourite things to do when I'm travelling is to try the local food and embrace the local culture and wear the local clothes. I'm fortunate that so far around the world I've managed to avoid the famed 'Delhi Belly' and am proud of my cast-iron stomach. I ate a lot of mutton, rice and bread in Afghanistan and not enough vegetables. On one occasion, I joined a band of men in the local restaurant (there were no women), sitting cross-legged on the floor over a low wooden table, all sharing food from large platters. It was probably quite unhygienic, sharing bread together. Some of the guys had been working all day and their hands were filthy. But I loved talking to strangers, engaging with them and trying to explain who I was and why I was in their country. Not many people spoke English, so it was quite entertaining at times. I enjoyed the communality of mealtimes with strangers mixing together and chatting away, doing various business deals. These deals were always sealed with a cup of sweet chai and the meals could go on for two or three hours at a time. Every twenty to thirty minutes a few more plates of food would arrive and off we'd go again. There seemed to be little concept of time. Everything was relaxed and daily life progressed at a slow and comfortable pace.

The more I interacted with the local Afghans, the more I realised how important it is for Westerners to put themselves in their shoes. We talk about how awful it is to live in a war zone, but in reality the people I met didn't see themselves as living in a war zone. They just saw themselves as living at home, in their own country. They were forced to accept the destruction and did their best to get on with it. In every war zone, there are children who are constantly drawn into the horrors and the suffering, but in every war zone there are also those brave and courageous people and organisations who are working to stop the underlying causes of conflict and support those children whose lives have been devastated by violence. Among the bombs and bullets, a lot of great humanitarian work is done by people pulling together.

As Westerners we're worried about who is going to get shot next, but for those living and working in conflict zones it seemed just part of their daily life and they got on with it. Kids still played in the streets, business got done, markets remained bustling, deals were sealed, groceries were bought and lives were lived until an incident happened and then all hell let loose and everyone scattered.

It's interesting how different cultures manage turmoil and what is acceptable for one culture appears strange and uncomfortable for another. When I was working as a military intelligence operator in Iraq back in 2005, my personal interpreter, Mohammed, kindly invited me to his house one day for food and to meet his family. Tacked to his wooden front door by its ears was the head of a sheep and there were rivers of bright red blood running from its slit throat. When Mohammed's young son opened the door to welcome me in, he too had blood all over his hands. It was a sort of sacrificial welcoming ceremony to say, 'Jordan, you're a special guest. Come on into our home.' It was incredible, the blood was running all down the pathway and the kid was running around barefoot. I could see little bloody footprints all over the floor. I said to my interpreter, 'Bloody hell, mate, this is fucking crazy, what's this about?' I was joking of course and having a bit of banter with him.

'Hey, it's just a different culture, mate, different culture,' he said.

'Nah, that's just weird.'

I was quite young and naïve at that time and wasn't up to speed with fully understanding cultural differences. He replied, 'No, Jordan, I'll tell you what's weird. Back in the late 1980s, when I was studying in the UK at Oxford University, I arrived at the end of October and someone knocks on my student accommodation with a frightening mask on and they're threatening me with tricks, asking me for money and trying to scare me.'

'You mean Halloween?' I laughed.

'Yes, I think that's what you crazy people call it over there. A week later, I was walking through London and there's a bonfire and they were putting a man in a suit on the top of it and setting off bombs and rockets and celebrating, like it was something funny. That's not funny.'

That little discussion did make me stop to think how crazy Halloween and Bonfire Night must look to someone who was unused to our country's customs. And that's just what I was guilty of – I went to his house and made an instant judgement because tacking a severed sheep's bloody head to my front door is not normal to me. That was my first introduction to how different our culture is. We see all these extreme nation-alist groups in the UK these days who spout anti-Muslim rhetoric, saying they shouldn't do this, that or the other in our country. So long as people respect each other and respect each other's cultures, it doesn't matter what country you're in. The most important thing is to have respect for other people and perhaps before we can do that, we must have self-respect too – respect and understanding.

Tragically, Mohammed, who had so kindly welcomed me into his home, sheep's head and all, and who was so movingly grateful for the tent and the few remaining possessions I gave him when I left Iraq, was murdered for helping the British forces after the troops pulled out. He was just one of the many Iraqis working as part of military–civilian cooperation. Others included not only interpreters, but cleaners on camp, waste disposers and informants. These guys were not well paid and were taking huge personal risks because their local communities often perceived them as working for the opposition forces. Many of these Iraqi workers were promised UK citizenship and family protection, but it never happened and they were ultimately betrayed. I heard several stories from local people who were still guarding the military bases when I was running in Iraq. Many of them had a bitter taste in their mouth about the way the coalition forces had abandoned those Iraqis who had done so much to help them. 'You didn't care for us. You got what you needed out of us and then you just washed your hands of us,' they said. 'We were told we would be looked after, our families might be protected, we'd get a visa.' They felt betrayed, and who could blame them?

CHAPTER SIXTEEN

BEAUTIFUL BAMIYAN

I spent four days in Bamiyan before the marathon acclimatising to the altitude. I would be running at about 11,000 feet, so it was important to get used to the physical and mental effects of functioning at that height. Sometimes called 'mountain sickness,' altitude sickness is a group of symptoms that can strike if you walk or climb to a higher elevation too quickly. The pressure of the air that surrounds you is called barometric pressure, and when you go to higher altitudes, this pressure drops and there is less oxygen available. If you live in a place that's located at a moderately high altitude, you get used to the air pressure, so altitude sickness wasn't too much of a problem for the locals. But if you travel to a place at a higher altitude than you're used to, it's best to remember your body needs time to adjust to the change in pressure. Any time you go above 8,000 feet, you're risking altitude sickness, so running at 11,000 feet was going to be a challenge before I even worried about the possibility of having to cope with a seizure.

There was one US athlete also competing in the Afghan marathon, who had experience of extreme races around the world, and who told me there are three kinds of altitude sickness: acute mountain sickness is the mildest form and it's very common. The symptoms can feel like the worst hangover ever. High-altitude pulmonary oedema is a build-up of fluid in the lungs that can be very dangerous and even life threatening. Then there is a condition called high-altitude cerebral oedema, which is the most severe form of altitude sickness and happens when there's fluid in the brain. The symptoms are pretty grim and include headache, dizziness, nausea, vomiting, fatigue and loss of energy, shortness of breath, trouble sleeping and loss of appetite. It's life threatening, so you have to seek immediate medical attention.

It was imperative I got my body used to the high altitude, so I went for a jog every morning on my own in the mountains. I was shocked at how exhausted I felt after just thirty seconds of running. My chest was tight as a drum and I was left gasping for breath, taking in huge lungfuls of the stuff. I was overcome with the terrible thought I might fail this leg of the expedition. Having to stop every few minutes just to draw breath didn't bode well for running my first ever full marathon. What the hell had I committed myself to? I wouldn't be able to just stop mid-marathon. I would have to push myself to keep going, come hell or high water.

The marathon itself began in the beautiful Afghan National Park. Band-e Amir is a couple of hours' drive from Bamiyan and was designated as Afghanistan's first national park in 2009. It's a series of six deep, bright blue lakes separated by natural dams made up of a mineral deposit called travertine. Apart from the stunning lakes, the landscape is rolling and featureless, but in the spring it greens up considerably and becomes home to flocks of nomads. As the road reaches the top of a hill, you first catch sight of the main lake of Band-e Amir. It's quite an astonishing sight to see this blue water peppered with the lushness of surrounding green shrubland. The amazing colour of the water is formed by the tinting of the mineral salts from the springs that feed the lake.

Early morning and the sun was out and shining. It was already thirty-one degrees and the temperature would get hotter as the day wore on. The altitude was already squeezing the oxygen from the air, making it difficult to breathe. Lined up at the starting point were at least 200 local runners, plus a smattering of foreigners; two Italians, an American, a Norwegian and a Swede. I was the only Brit. It was just such an incredible sight to see all these runners. The race was open to anyone who wanted to run – women, men, teenagers. Women are often treated like second-class citizens in Afghanistan, so to see them running alongside men was eye-opening. For

26.2 miles, all the runners were treated equally. I could see how much it all meant to the people hosting the event.

Despite the challenging terrain and the sheer horror of the heat and altitude, everyone pulled together and supported each other. For people who had been worn down by war, they were truly remarkable. They were so open and welcoming to me, a man essentially a stranger in their midst. On the day of the race, there was a big influx of police from different provinces who had come to secure the area. There was also a military presence, including armed police and special forces, which I was pleased to see. Had there been any trouble, we would have been well protected, although I'm sure they weren't there for my personal benefit.

I have to be honest and admit that the actual run itself was the toughest thing I've ever done in my life both physically and mentally. It was far, far worse than I expected. I was sweating excessively, the salt running straight down my forehead and into my eyes, making them sting. My eyes felt like they had been attacked with pepper spray. My whole face was on fire. And then the nosebleeds started. Every couple of miles my nose would dribble blood. It would mix with the sweat on my upper lip and gather in the corners of my mouth. The taste was nasty, kind of salty and metallic. The salt in my sweat began to irritate the skin under my left eye and I rubbed it so hard for relief, the thin skin began to crack. The altitude was not the only antagonist, the wind was a killer too. To prevent any further windburn on my reddened, sore skin, I kept my face hidden behind a neck scarf with just my eyes on show. Keeping my hat stuck firmly on my head was a challenge in the fierce wind, but thankfully it had a built-in necessary neck protector. As I plodded along I became aware of my blistered feet burning in my running shoes. The thought of plunging them into a cold basin of water kept me going. But when my thighs began to chafe I thought I'd really had it!

About halfway through the run, at roughly the ten- or twelve-mile mark, I got a desperate urge to take a shit. Bloody awful timing, but what could I do? I remember seeing Paula Radcliffe squat by the side of the road and take a pee when she was running in the London Marathon. I felt bad for her, but when you gotta go, you gotta go. I was desperate and knew I wouldn't be able to make it for another few hours. But I was concerned because there were women running in this race and I couldn't just squat down and take a dump in front of them. I'd have to be more discreet and get off the road. The terrain had been uphill and downhill, one hill after another. I thought if I can just make it up over this hill I can find a place in the valley to squat. But every time I got to the top of a hill, I'd turn and see another runner, usually a woman, right behind me. Not a protective bush in sight, just acres and acres of brown sand, dust and desert. I was getting gut ache, and was killing myself for about half a mile trying to get as close as I could to the person in front in order to leave a massive gap before the person behind. I needed to time it perfectly to get the whole mountain to myself. Never had a shit been so complicated to accomplish. When glorious relief eventually came I realised I had no toilet paper. I had to rip off and use the bottom half of my neck scarf.

Even though we were running in the middle of nowhere, the mountainous route took me through lots of small villages. As I passed through, all the children came out from their homes to cheer me and the other runners on. Apparently, when the first runners came through the kids were rather bewildered, not fully understanding what was going on. But by the time the other slower runners and I ran through their village, they were high-fiving us and throwing us sweets.

I ran along dirt tracks, through desert and sand, up mountains, down mountains, past rolling hills, by lakes and sandstone ruins and past shepherds herding their flocks. All of a sudden I'd go over a hill and come down the other side to be greeted by five or six mud huts with a line of washing and an old woman cooking outside with her pot by a bonfire. There were very few stone buildings, everything was as basic as could be. Every so often, what passed for an Afghan ambulance would go by, more of a rusty old 4x4 with a medical symbol on the side. Sitting inside, I saw various runners who couldn't take the pace and pain any more and who had dropped out of the race. I longed to join them! But seeing the faces on the village children reminded me exactly why I had chosen to run these three races in the first place. I wasn't going to stop now. They were the reason I was putting myself through this hell. I knew it was going to take me a long time to finish the race, but even if it meant crawling across the finish line, there was no way after coming all the way to Afghanistan that I was not going to complete it. I knew I just had to keep putting one foot in front of the other. Just keep plodding on, looking forward to the next watering hole.

Seven hours after starting the race, I was no longer plodding; my feet were simply scraping the ground in a mad stumbling fashion and blowing up a fat trail of dust behind me. The relief as I lurched over the finishing line, clutching my sides, was intense. Being one of the later runners to finish, some of the ones who had already completed ran alongside me for the final 400 metres, encouraging and cheering me on. Cue more high-fives, wide smiles and plenty of back-slapping. Less than half of the original runners had managed to complete the course. Several of the runners had succumbed to altitude sickness. One of the professional international runners said, 'I've run all over the world and that's the toughest race I've ever run in.' As the organiser put the medal of completion round my neck, I remember thinking, 'I've bloody done something here.' I felt an enormous sense of fulfilment. I think it was probably one of the proudest things I've done from a physical perspective; it was by far the toughest race I've completed. Still, I hadn't bottled it, and as far as I was concerned – for an injured veteran with a bad back, epilepsy, anxiety and severe depression – it was one hell of an achievement and I was extremely proud to be there, experiencing this special moment. I was very emotional to be honest.

Back at my accommodation, I was gagging for a beer, but I just had a nice glass of water with some lemon and ice instead. It wasn't necessary to talk to anyone about what I'd achieved. It was knowing that I'd done something incredible for a good purpose and cause that mattered. I didn't feel that I needed to celebrate with anyone else, I just wanted to be alone, to breathe it all in and suck it up. I felt happy in my own skin and totally at peace with myself – a feeling I had not had for many years. This was the pinnacle of everything that I'd been striving for done, everything that I'd been working towards for the past couple of years and everything that I wanted. Personally, I felt a huge sense of achievement and relief. I'd gained a sense of purpose that I wanted to hang on to, expand and take with me into the future. I felt buoyed up and full of positivity, a feeling that I wanted to embrace tightly. Yes, I was tired, drained and exhausted, but I also felt like I was on top of the world. I was riding high on an incredibly special moment. I was right there in the 'now', surrounded by peace and tranquillity. I had no access to any internet service or social media and was blissfully disconnected from the wider world. I was living life on my terms for that short time and my only small regret was that Evie was not there to share that beautiful moment with me.

Afghanistan has seen huge progress with the help of its Western allies in transforming itself in less than twenty years from the horrors of Taliban rule to an emerging parliamentary democracy and a trading link between the East and the West, but there is a long way to go yet. Sadly, a few weeks after I left Afghanistan and returned home to the UK, I read that British military veteran from Merseyside, Luke Griffin, who had worked for the security firm G4S for eight years, had been killed in a Taliban attack in Kabul. G4S provides security for clients including the British Embassy and other companies and organisations working in Afghanistan. Taliban insurgents had attacked the G4S compound by blasting a car bomb outside the premises and gaining access to the inside. Four Afghans working for the company were also killed. Several hundred people then took refuge in surrounding bunkers purpose-built for any such incident, while Afghan commandos attempted the clear the compound of any remaining fighters. The damage done to the compound was massive, leaving a huge glaring crater slap bang in the middle. The surrounding buildings were completely destroyed.

Both the Taliban and ISIS have increased their attacks on Kabul, which is thought to be one of the deadliest places in Afghanistan for civilians. The security services are no strangers to managing insurgent attacks. In March 2019, a Taliban car bomb killed three people and wounded two in Kabul in an attack on a G4S vehicle, but in this instance the suicide bomber detonated himself before actually reaching his intended target. The year 2018 was considered the dead-liest year of the West's seventeen-year-long effort to support the Afghan government against the Taliban and the Afghan city of Kabul has become the focus for much of the violence in recent years. My experience in Baghdad, I'm happy to say, had been quite different to what goes on in Kabul. Yes, Baghdad has its inherent dangers, but to this day I'm truly amazed at how the local population remain so welcoming and content-ed with their lot, even though they never really know what's around the corner and whether that day might be their last on earth.

On International Women's Day recently, I read that the women of Afghanistan marked the day with a public holiday. They were asking for time to reflect on their futures under possible Taliban rule if the group were once again successful in their quest to return. The US President Donald Trump was aiming to end the long war in Afghanistan with a so-called 'peace process' and was withdrawing troops ahead of a pos-sible bid for re-election in 2020. Unfortunately, the result of this is the Taliban now have a global platform as a legitimate political force. Even though the Taliban are claiming to protect women's rights, it doesn't bode well for Afghan women. They are frightened of being forced to return to the old days of violence and marginalisation. They could see their new-found liberation eroding before their very eyes. The thought of all the women I had met in Afghanistan having their identity and their very existence ripped from them is unsupportable to me.

Life is particularly hard for Afghan women. Tens of thousands have been made widows since the war was created. When their husbands are killed, they are left to raise their families alone in a country with a chronic lack of economic opportunity. Even worse, a new widow must rely entirely on her husband's immediate family for support, which often means she is forced to marry the next available brother or cousin. I can't imagine the dread these women must feel at the thought of being passed around the men in the family like a parcel.

The majority of Afghanis desperately want peace, but not at any cost. Many of those displaced by the fighting, especially those living in rural areas, already lack the basic rights that those in the cities are so afraid of losing. On my return to the UK, I read an article about an Afghan family who had been forced from their chicken farm after the Taliban had bombed it and taken all their chickens. Apparently, the blasts were so fierce that the four-year-old son developed bleeding stress blisters on his lips. The poor boy would hide under his father's shirt for comfort.

The Afghans now seem to be facing a moral dilemma. On the one hand there are those living in urban areas who are cautioning against a rushed deal with the Taliban that could put women's rights to work and education in jeopardy, and then there are those in more rural areas who are already deprived of schools, institutions and the basic necessities of life who want peace. Many of the schools built in the early years after the Taliban were toppled, when things were more hopeful, have since been destroyed in combat. They remain practically derelict, their walls riddled with bullets. And it's these schools that are often taken over by armed men because there is little infrastructure that is useable. Those displaced by the fighting seem desperate for any kind of peace deal. I'm sure they don't feel they have much more to lose and are simply focused on staying alive.

Back at home, I was invited to do an interview with the BBC. The presenter looked me in the eye and with a serious voice said, 'It's incredibly dangerous and risky running through these war zones. People get killed in these places. Weren't you worried about putting yourself and others in danger?'

'No, what's quite incredible is the fact that I've just run the Afghanistan marathon with lots of people, all of whom were smiling and happy and I didn't see anyone shooting anybody,' I said. 'I didn't see anyone getting murdered or killed, but the moment I landed back in the UK and switched on the news, I heard about three shootings in London and two stabbings in Manchester, yet we're so focused on what's going on in other parts of the world. I had an incredible time in Afghanistan. In fact, in all three countries I was shown so much respect. I was welcomed. Yes, there were elements of danger and risk, that's why the project was named Running Dangerously, but I didn't feel any more at risk than walking through the centre of London on a dark night. It was all managed professionally.'

Unbelievably and somewhat ironically, a few months after this interview, I read a story in a British national newspaper that Somali mothers living in north London are now sending their children back to Somalia and Somaliland because the north London Somali community believe the police can no longer protect their teenagers from county line gangs and rampant knife crime. Representatives from this community say hundreds of children have been flown back because of rising concerns over drug gangs and the criminal networks that use children to transport drugs from cities to the provinces.

Personally, I believe that if you continually assess the risk and understand the complexity of the challenges you face, you are engaging in effective due diligence. I could have run in Mogadishu without any problems and I might have been all right. I might have got away with it. But after Abdi told me not to, it made me think twice. After all, the guy had lived there for the last forty years and he knew the place like the back of his hand. It would have been very easy for me to ignore his advice and just do it anyway, because that's what we do as Brits. We can be quite arrogant and ignorant sometimes. But you learn over time, and the more you embrace other people's cultures and the more you travel the world, the more you get to know who's talking shite and who's talking sense. I think there's a lot to be said for standing in front of somebody and looking at them in the white of their eyes to see what they're all about. When Abdi looked me in the eye, it was serious business and it was important I listened. God bless his soul.

CHAPTER SEVENTEEN

BE THE DIFFERENCE THAT MAKES A DIFFERENCE

The Running Dangerously expedition was a journey during which I learned a lot. I had been transformed from a soldier taking orders from above and being part of a strong group identity, to a man completely in charge of his own destiny who made individual choices. Life may be one long lesson, but I think the most important thing to learn is to understand yourself and what makes you tick. With hindsight, I now realise my priorities in life had been wrong for many years. The things I'd tried to chase, the things I perceived to be of value, were all completely the opposite to what I now believe are important. It's been an interesting 180-degree flip. I'd always wanted to be successful, but my understanding of success was to drive a nice car, to live in a big house, to hang out with cool people. But actually, I couldn't give a shit about any of those things any more. The kind of people I looked up to and admired five years ago are not the same people I respect today. The people who I admire today are the people who are making a difference in the world and not just the people who are making money for the sake of it. The people I now admire are living personally fulfilling and enriching lives – the humanitarians, the NGO workers, the people living in camps in the middle of nowhere, the explorers, the adventurers, the pioneers, the people who are giving back to society and humankind in so many different ways.

My journey had taken me to some incredible places. It was a journey full of twists and turns, ups and downs, despair and hope. I'd met some of the most admirable and big-hearted people, from the wonderful characters in three of the most dangerous places on the planet, to all the people around the world who had so generously supported me in my fundraising and planning efforts. The loss of my new friend Abdi had tinged the expedition with sadness, but I think he would have been proud of our efforts to raise money for children's education in his homeland.

In reality, the whole expedition was a team effort from the sponsors and the donors to the organisers, the supporters, the media and the other runners. Everyone made a huge investment of time, effort, resources and love. Collectively, we achieved a great deal and I'm proud of the fact that every pound or dollar raised that goes into our expedition pot goes directly to charity. None of the money we raised then, or continue to raise now, goes on salaries, logistics or administration costs.

The project raised over £100,000, which was distributed among the various charities associated with the expedition, with War Child in the UK and US being the largest beneficiaries of the project. War Child do some incredible work, particularly in Iraq and Afghanistan where their main focus is standing up for the rights of children, safeguarding them and providing them with access to basic educational resources. They work with local communities and families to help find and protect unaccompanied minors, children working on the streets and those who come from extremely disadvantaged backgrounds, and they are highly commendable.

However, one of the major challenges and obstacles for me personally, when working with the larger charities, was that it's very difficult as a fundraiser or donor to keep a track of where exactly the funds you have provided have gone. I appreciate that there are lots of processes and procedures to go through for compliance, and of course the children in many cases need their identities protected for security reasons, and rightly so, but I wish there was a way for charities to work more closely with donors so that we can understand where every single penny goes. I think this is really important. It was for this reason I set up a charity called Frontline Children with some fellow trustees, which consists of a small group of volunteers working to inspire hope and change lives in war and conflict regions through education and opportunity. At present no member of staff at Frontline Children is paid a salary at all. This is what charity is all about for me – giving not getting. Saying that, however, I do understand that working with only volunteers can perhaps limit the growth and indeed the impact of the charity. Personally, I find it far more transparent and ethical knowing that every penny raised goes directly to where it needs to be and that every penny or cent raised helps the children who directly need it. I'm proud that Running Dangerously and all its supporters are guaranteeing the futures of dispossessed children in terms of their orphanage fees, their education and funds for their teachers. Our main intention now is to build a school in Djibouti for the refugees who have been displaced by the wars in Yemen and Somalia. We will do our best to maintain a dialogue and monitor the progress of our outcomes.

But one of the main results of the expedition was far more personal to me. I took the opportunity to look in the mirror and reflect on what I had lost… and gone on to find. Back on that rooftop in Dubai I'd lost sight of all that really mattered to me. I had no grip on my life, my values and my family. I'd forgotten who I was, I'd forgotten my duty and I'd forgotten the values the army and my parents had instilled in me. It's not in the power of everyone to make a difference, but it is in the power of many. It's not clever to go through life thinking somebody else will pick up the pieces and make everything all right. We have to give it a go ourselves. If we all try to give a little, we can do a lot, I'm sure of that now.

There's no doubt in my mind that actually going out and doing something bigger and better than me has helped my mental health beyond anything I'd hoped. I am in a better place mentally, physically and emotionally and I know I need to carry on looking for another challenge to keep up the momentum. I need more mental and physical stimulation to see me through the next chapter of my life. I've spent the majority of my life in the military or in the maritime security industries. Being able to make a difference in children's lives has opened something up inside me. It's been a doorway to a future that requires me to think less about my own troubles and more about service to others. To be perfectly honest, I don't really enjoy running extreme long distances. It's not my first port of call for 'challenging entertainment'. When I crossed the finish line in Afghanistan after about seven hours of punishing running, just sitting there at the side of the road looking into the mountains, I remember thinking, 'Bloody hell, that's been such an incredible journey to go from Somalia to Somaliland to Iraq, to now sitting here in Afghanistan.' I was gazing at the mountains beyond when I noticed a couple of children playing, skipping around. I realised that even though it was the end of that particular journey for me, it was just the start of something much bigger. I decided there and then that I was going to dedicate a lot more of my time and future to helping other people. Being able to do something impactful was personally healing and I was grateful for the opportunity.

The Running Dangerously project showed me that children growing up and living in war zones have a magical way of learning to adjust to whatever life throws at them. They are truly resilient and I hope these experiences will give them the skills they need to adjust to constant change in their young lives and to focus on what they need to move forward. When I was out in Somalia, Iraq and Afghanistan, I chose to focus on the beauty and the love around me and tried to block out the bullet holes, the bombs and the threats. I needed to focus on positive thoughts and not allow the thoughts of conflict to control me. Building my resilience has allowed me to manage my stress and overlook the negative events in my life. During the expedition, I learned even more powerfully the value of putting materialistic things into perspective. Material things can disappear as quickly as they are acquired and are of comparatively little value. None of the people I met on my travels possessed anything remotely valuable in material terms. But they all possessed a wealth of courage and spirit.

The expedition also taught me the importance of stopping to take time out to reflect and to take the lessons that reflection offers. I don't think it's helpful to dwell on our mistakes; they are in the past and there is nothing we can do to change them. We can only learn from them and move forward. When it comes to depression and mental health, we're often battling with ourselves and with the demons in our own head. The only way to counter this is by focusing on the positives and by moving forward. I will never know what the outcome would have been if I hadn't taken the phone call from Mum up on that rooftop in Dubai, but I do remember that it was the lowest I have ever felt in my entire life. That's why I now always try to surround myself with positive people who are prepared to listen and offer support. Listening is one of those skills that's massively undervalued in life. Sometimes it's all we need; somebody just to vent too, somebody who's not going to judge you, not have an opinion of you, but just listen and absorb.

As well as the importance of reflection, the expedition also hammered home the importance of planning. Failing to plan is planning to fail. The concept of planning is critical to me, but the ability to stick to the plan is not necessary paramount to success by any means. No plan survives first contact with the enemy, as we used to say in the army, but when the shit hits the fan, you must have a plan B and possibly a plan C for extra back-up. The Running Dangerously project confirmed this for me. Logistically, it was a nightmare, and things didn't quite pan out the way I intended, but somehow it all came right in the end. We had a method in the army – we called it 'actions on', where before going on operations or on exercise, we would agree several considerations with our platoon or troop. What are the actions on if we see the enemy? What are the actions on if we get lost? What are the actions on if the patrol is compromised? What are the actions on if someone in our team gets shot or injured? In this way, everyone agrees what the actions on are before the event happens. I carried this actions on habit during the expedition and also with my everyday life after leaving the army. I often go through different scenarios in my head and if anything stresses me out I play out the 'what ifs' in my mind.

I believe that informed choices, decisions and accountability are everything in life. Every action you take in life, work or relationships has a reaction, and it's important to remember this. When I forgot this basic premise back in 2015, my world fell apart. Every decision you make will have a consequence of some sort, whether it's shooting at the enemy on the battlefield, running through a dangerous country, or arguing with your partner in love or business. We are the architects of our own destinies in this world. When I was younger I just did things and dealt with the shit afterwards, but as I got older I became a better risk manager. I make a point now of telling young guys in the schools and the colleges I am invited to speak at that when you do something naughty as a youngster, half of what's exciting is telling your friends the story in shocking detail. As you grow older you learn to live with your own conscience and you're quite at peace in your mind. I tell them that a wise man learns from his mistakes, but a wiser man learns from the mistakes of others. Use me as your example, I tell them, because I was the person who was messing around in school twenty years ago. I was the guy who didn't turn up for his exams. I was the potential failure.

The Running Dangerously expedition made a profound impact on my psychological health and I've noticed that the issue of mental health always seems to interest people. At a talk I was giving recently at the UK National Running Show at the NEC in Birmingham, I was asked by a member of the audience, 'What's the best medicine for depression?'

'I've been on 100 milligrams of Sertraline, fifty milligrams and twenty-five milligrams,' I replied, 'but there's no better drug in the world than running.' That statement was greeted with an unexpectedly rapturous cheer. But then everyone was clapping because the audience was mostly made up of runners and they totally got the power of running and exercise. I told the audience that we may not have the power to change an experience, because an experience is what it is, but what we do have is the power to change *how* we experience that experience. You can let those dark voices in your head overwhelm you and have a bad day, or you can make the voices focus on all the good stuff and it turns out to be a pretty wonderful day. And, guess what? It's still the exact same day. A happy, positive runner performs better and feels more satisfaction. Big leaps can happen when you run. You can transform your body as well as your mind, but these transformations only occur over time, so patience and commitment are necessary.

I achieved a great sense of fulfilment from running. Fulfilment is different from success. There were no crowds cheering me on when I went over the finishing lines in Iraq and Afghanistan. It was just me plodding along on my own. To me, success is more tangible, it depends on others recognising your achievements and the fact you've done something great. Fulfilment is far more intrinsic, far more personal and far more valuable. At the beginning of the Running Dangerously expedition, not completing the runs would have felt like a failure to me, but looking back there was never a risk of failure because so many good things came out of the project. Saying that, at no time was it ever in my mind that I would not complete the challenges. It was more than my own sense of pride at stake. I had the sponsors and the donors to think about. They were kind enough to give so much in terms of money and kit and paying for flights and accommodation. Obviously, they all want good PR at the end of the runs and to be able to say, 'Jordan finished the marathon of Afghanistan,' and not, 'Oh, he was that guy who tried, but failed.'

I think there's a lot of good to be said for giving back. I found myself in a much healthier place from helping others. In my early years, I admit I was really quite selfish and self-centred.

Before I joined the army I was all about what's in it for me, what can I get out of this? Whereas now I try to approach life with a mindset of how can I help you? What can I do for you? How can I use my network, my skills, my expertise, to help you? I find that by having that approach, life is reciprocal and things are drawn to you. I don't know if it's karma, or if it's positive vibes, or the universe responding. Five years ago, I'd have said, 'What a load of bullshit.' Now, I'm beginning to believe that what goes around, comes around. What you give out, you get back. The reward may not be immediate. It may take some time, but you'll recognise it when it comes. However, saying that, I feel disappointed in myself that I didn't work as hard as I should have when I was younger, because now I play to win.

During my daughter's sports day in 2018, I was standing on the sidelines and giving her a pep talk ready for her 100-metre sprint. The PE teacher was standing right behind me. 'Come on, Evie, come on,' I said. 'This is your race, come on, focus on winning now.'

'Yeah, I'm going to, Daddy. I'll do my very best to win, Daddy.'

'Remember, you have to win. Think: I've got to win. I must win.'

The PE teacher was not very happy with that. After Evie left for the starting line, he popped his head over my shoulder and said, 'Is it Mr Wylie? May I have a quick word with you?'

Then he pulled me aside. 'I don't want to offend you,' he said, 'but I don't think you should be talking to your daughter in that manner. You're emphasising how important winning is.'

'OK. So what's the problem with that? Why is that a big issue for you?' I asked.

'Well, winning isn't the most important thing, it's the taking part that's important. We're trying to build a community spirit in the school. Everyone who takes part will get a sticker and be made to feel special.'

'So, what happened to gold, silver and bronze then?' I asked.

'That's not what we're about. We're about inclusion here, Mr Wylie,' he replied.

'I understand your logic and your reasoning, but I think that is what's wrong with society today. Everyone's rewarded just for taking part. We're not equals in life and it pays to be a winner. I believe we should all strive and do our best to be winners.'

'OK,' he countered, 'what if she doesn't win today, how do you think she's going to feel?'

'Then we take the lessons from that,' I replied.

I respect winners, but I also respect those who are magnanimous in defeat. I take inspiration from people who are trying to do incredible things. I surround myself with people who are often super-fit, who have done crazy adventures. The Bremont Adventurers Club, of which I am a member, is full of incredible people, including Olympians, adventurers and world-record holders. These are the people I want to associate with and surround myself with. Most of them have more medals than me and have won more records than me, but they're the people who inspire me to want to be a better version of myself. I believe that if you find yourself in a group of opposite-minded people, people who don't reflect your values, then that becomes a reflection of you and of what you're prepared to accept. Most people will talk a good game, but people who actually deliver are rare.

As well as a desire to win, having a sense of purpose is important in my life. For me, a sense of purpose is far more than just having good intentions. The long days and evenings of toil, the disappointments and the setbacks, the struggle and the sacrifice are all worth it, because ultimately the efforts pay dividends to other people. At its core, the idea of purpose is the idea that what we do matters to people other than ourselves. But having said that, I'm no altruist. I was helping my mental health via the project at the same time as helping others. When I take a moment to reflect on the times in my life when I've been at my best and risen to the challenges before me and found the strength to do what might have seemed impossible, I realise the goals that I have achieved were connected in some way, shape or form to the benefit of other people. A sense of purpose is not some fully formed thing that you find out of the blue. It's much more dynamic than that. Whether you clean houses, fix cars, or run a multimillion-pound company for a living, think about how it connects to the bigger picture and how it can be an expression of your deeper values. Ultimately, although a life filled with purpose is difficult and full of frustrations and obstacles, it's also enormously gratifying. But seeing that someone needs our help isn't enough. There must be a conviction, an intent to take action. You have to believe that your actions will not be in vain.

I always need to be working towards something. I can't just plod along through life willy-nilly and just go day-by-day. I have to have short-, medium- and long-term goals. Every single day I plot and plan a way towards achieving them. Every single day I measure my progress towards getting closer to my goals. The military instilled in me that planning and preparation is everything, but I think growing up and maturing and being open to learning new things and skills is also life-enhancing. We all have setbacks and everyone has challenges, hurdles and obstacles to overcome, but the beauty of them is they all teach you about yourself. Routine is far more dangerous than risk. Do what makes you happy and focus on the here and now. Live in the moment and add life to your days rather than days to your life. Winning and being successful are great – embracing the glory is great, but it's the small failures that teach you the biggest lessons. Failure can make you stop, reflect, look in the mirror and say, 'OK, maybe we didn't get it right this time. What do we now need to do differently?' All I know for sure is that I've never been a superstar fitness machine or anything remotely like it, and if I didn't have any project or expedition to work towards, I'd probably lie on the couch all day watching footy and eating Doritos.

I admire people who are relentless in pursuit of their goals and do whatever it takes to achieve them. Society attaches too much stigma to different types of people based on social status, religion, culture or education. Young people today are so heavily influenced by social media telling them what they can and cannot achieve. I tell young people they can achieve anything they want. I talk quite a lot about my own personal journey and how things like core values are important. They are important because they provide the tools and the skills and the attributes necessary to achieve what you want in life. If you respect people, if you're selfless, if you have integrity at the core of everything you do, if you're disciplined – nothing can stop you. Having discipline is a big requirement, because to achieve an adventure or expedition, you have to be very disciplined, not only in your fitness regime, but also in your personal and social life. Sometimes you need to be prepared to cut aspects of it out altogether while you're on your mission. It takes dedication and, above all, sacrifice. Nothing worth doing comes easy. If you want to achieve something that's never been done before, you've got to do something that's never been done before to achieve it. Many of us quit what we start far too early and far too often. What matters is that we wake up day after day and get on that treadmill whether we feel like it or not. Eighty per cent of success in life is showing up, as far as I've learned.

The other necessary component to making a difference in this world is courage. The people I met along the way had bags of it. We are all fearful of the unknown, but courage is knowing what not to fear. Fear occurs when we interpret a threat as something that's going to cause us pain or discomfort and we feel we have no control over it. Fear makes us feel we have no defence over the way anxiety, distress, panic or disease takes hold of our mental, physical and emotional body. Courage begins with a choice not to let fear rule our life and is the first step we take to making decisions about our future. Courage is based on trust in our greater purpose and recognition that we are equipped with all the tools necessary to handle any situation with realistic expectations. Courage is moving towards our own development and growth, not because of fear, but in spite of it. In my Running Dangerously journey, I met many people full of fear and many people full of immense courage. Both the fearful and the courageous have the power to change lives. When we live courageously, we lead with integrity and passion, inspiring others around us to do the same, we make a positive impact on our community and around the world and we open ourselves up to vulnerability to experience life in the present moment.

From courage comes grit and determination. I like to

think of grit as passion and perseverance for long-term and meaningful goals. I lead a goal-oriented life because I need goals to function. In all honesty, I'd far rather go down the pub with my mates. Long-term goals are my north star, and underpin everything I do. I see grit and determination as important drivers of achievement and success, independent of talent and intelligence. In other words, you don't have to be a brainbox to have grit and determination. Without grit, talent is useless. It's only with effort that talent leads to success.

To this end, I'm harnessing all my grit and determination to plan my latest expedition to raise funds for children living in conflict zones. It's a continuation of the danger theme. Again, I will be pushing the boundaries of physical, psychological and emotional endurance. I wouldn't say I'm particularly attracted to danger and, as I've tried to put across, any danger I potentially put myself in is based on a strict and uncompromising risk assessment, but I'm aware that having a danger theme to the project sparks a lot of interest and makes it more compelling. When you're working on a charity project, you need fundraising, donors, sponsors, media interest and PR activity, and they are not interested in supporting a run around the park or a quick tandem dive out of a two-seater plane. And danger and risk are no strangers to me; I've lived and breathed them both for the past twenty years. Strangely, I feel quite comfortable when I'm in remote, hostile and complex environments. To me, it's no different to accountants working with a bunch of spreadsheets in a back office. I enjoy managing risk in extreme circumstances. It's fascinating to leverage one set of risks against another. I also enjoy challenging people's perceptions. Nothing is more appealing in terms of adventure to me than when someone says it can't be done, or it's never been done before. I just want to prove them wrong and show that it can be done if the risks are managed securely. Yes, I can be bloody-minded and stubborn.

I've harvested all my thoughts and feelings about grit, resilience, positivity, challenge and goal-setting to get my new fundraising expedition over the horizon. This particular project is called 'Rowing Dangerously' and, as the title suggests, it not about running this time – but rowing. I'm planning to row solo, unarmed, unsupported and unassisted across the most dangerous stretch of water in the world in November 2019, and I hope by the time you are reading this book, I will have already safely accomplished this incredible world first. If I fail, have a seizure or am captured by pirates, no doubt you will hear about it.

The Bab-El-Mandeb Straits is a shark-infested strip of water full of armed pirates just waiting to seize commercial ships, crews, and crazy British rowers for ransom. The 'Gate of Tears', as it translates to, is one of the busiest shipping lanes in the world, so it's not just pirates and sharks I will have to look out for. Any huge tanker minding its own business will be unable to see me out there rowing on the water. I will remain a tiny blip out at sea. There will also be the possibility of terrorists and armed smugglers to contend with. I'm excited, I'm apprehensive, but most of all I'm eager to raise more awareness and funds to help children living in conflict zones around the world. No person on record has ever attempted to row this notorious stretch of water solo, but I will. Saying that, I've never actually rowed a boat anywhere in my life yet, but I'm up for the challenge. Bring it on.

ABOUT THE AUTHOR

Jordan Wylie is former British soldier, extreme adventurer and philanthropist. Starting from humble beginnings, Jordan grew up on a council estate in Blackpool, Lancashire, and left school with no qualifications. After joining the British Army at sixteen years old, he served for ten years as a specialist in intelligence, surveillance and armoured reconnaissance,

RUNNING FOR MY LIFE

until an injury sustained in service meant his military career was cut short. He has worked in many of the world's most remote, hostile and complex environments and has diced with death on several occasions. Jordan has faced many personal challenges in recent years, including being diagnosed with severe depression, anxiety, epilepsy and dengue fever, as well as suffering the breakdown of his family. Despite these issues, Jordan continues to inspire everyone he crosses paths with and is perhaps best known for his roles as an ambassador, trustee and fundraiser for several international charities. Jordan has raised over a million pounds for charity and uses his profile as one of the stars of Channel 4's BAFTA-nominated shows *Hunted* and *Celebrity Hunted* to make a difference to children's lives worldwide, inspiring hope through education and access to opportunity.